Introduction

Chapter One; The Great Divide

Chapter Two; Why Are You Doing This, Anyway.

Chapter Three; Plays Well With Others.

Chapter Four; Rhythm; We'll Make A Drummer Out Of You Yet.

Chapter Five; To Read Or Not To Read.

Chapter Six; Sharps and Flats

Chapter Seven; Key Signatures and Scales

Chapter Eight; Basic Chord Theory

Chapter Nine; The Qualities

Chapter 10; Determining the Qualities of Three Note Chords

Chapter 11; Key Signatures and the Circle of Fifths.

Chapter 12; Chord Progressions, Melodies and Phrases.

Chapter 13; Improvisation, Jazz, Blues and Other Scales.

Chapter 14; Musical Forms

Chapter 15; Interpretation, Dynamics and Articulation.

Chapter 16; Crossing the Great Divide

Glossary

Introduction

An area where people quite often run into trouble with their music theory is tackling a particular level too soon. This is also known as skipping a gradient.

A gradient is when you present a subject of study at its most simple stage and then proceed to gradually add complexities. When doing this, in actual study, one must be certain to have nailed a level before going on to the next.

People who have studied learning have actually said that virtually anyone can learn a subject if the above rule is followed. Often, in music study, students will pick up a music theory book where the author makes the assumption that the reader is already familiar with some of the terms that he is using. This leads to frustration, confusion and the student soon gives up hope of understanding the subject. They put the book away thinking that the subject of theory is just too difficult to grasp. Here is a basic guide to a gradient approach to music theory;

1. Note types
2. Basic Rhythm and Beat
3. Reading notes on Treble or Bass Clef
4. Intervals
5. Scales
6. Sharps, Flats, Whole Steps and Half Steps
7. Key Signatures
8. Chords
9. Chord Inversions
10. Primary Chords
11. Chord Qualities
12. Minor Scales
13. Other Scale Types.

A good teacher will make sure their teaching is on a gradient for each particular student and also make sure the student fully understands each level before proceeding to the next. The other thing is to make sure you clear up any music definitions that you don't understand.

If you observe this rule of going by a gradient, your study of music theory will be easy and it will help you in your playing immensely.

Careful thought has been given to presenting the material in the correct gradient in this book. All the musical terms are explained and there is a glossary in the back of the book.

This book is intended as a supplement to regular lessons on your instrument. It's just that, as I explain in the book, some or more of these basics get dropped out or they are tackled in the wrong order and the music study suffers for it.

Use this book and follow the advice for study in it and you will succeed in learning to play music.

Visit www.gurusofmusic.com for more advanced study.

About the Author

Dizzy O'Brian went to the Peabody conservatory of Music in Baltimore, which is one of the top ranked music schools in the country. He is a performer and composer, whose unique style of pop Classical Fusion continues to grow in popularity.

Visit www.dizzyobrian.com to find out more about the music of Dizzy O'Brian.

Chapter One; The Great Divide

Probably everyone is familiar with the theory of the right brain and the left-brain. The theory goes that the left side of the brain handles logical sorts of things such as mathematics, while the right side of the brain is more intuitive and connected to the emotions.

A person will often be able to tell you what side of his brain is the dominant one. It is often offered as a bit of brag and also an excuse as to why they are always late or something.

Interestingly, if you take a look around the music scene, you can spot musicians and even musical genres that seem to be more right brained or left-brained.

This seems to hold true despite the fact that the theory says music is processed in the right brain. I don't doubt this but I think you will see my point about musicians and musical genres appearing to be either right brained or left-brained as we go on.

An example of a left-brained musician would be a 'classical' musician who reads music very well and plays rather pedantically. He cannot improvise and is terrified to do so. Changing the written note is something akin to heresy. It's a matter of pride that the music he plays is highly complex and he is a bit of a snob, looking down his nose at jazz or pop music and saying it's simple and crude.

An example of a right-brained musician would be a 'jazz' musician who 'plays by ear,' refuses to learn to read and protests vehemently if that is suggested. It's a matter of pride that his ear is so good that he doesn't need to learn to read music. He looks down on classical music as being for stuffed shirts. I think of the line from Star Wars when Hans Solo says 'Never tell me the odds!'

Now these two examples are extremes at either end of the divide we are discussing and I'm certainly not suggesting that all classical musicians or all jazz musicians fit these profiles.

It also appears that there are musical genres, which are more right-brained or left-brained. Easy to see how the so called classical music could be considered more of a left brain genre, especially with the Avant-garde music of the fifties and early sixties often being generated off of a mathematical formula.

If you've spent much time around the music scene, you have either encountered these extremes or you can identify with them.

It is also kind of easy to see that, if this theory is true, there are both positive and negative aspects to being more dominant on one side than the other, especially as far as being a musician is concerned.

If you've had trouble learning music or have encountered blocks to your progress, you can chalk it up to one or more of these negative aspects.

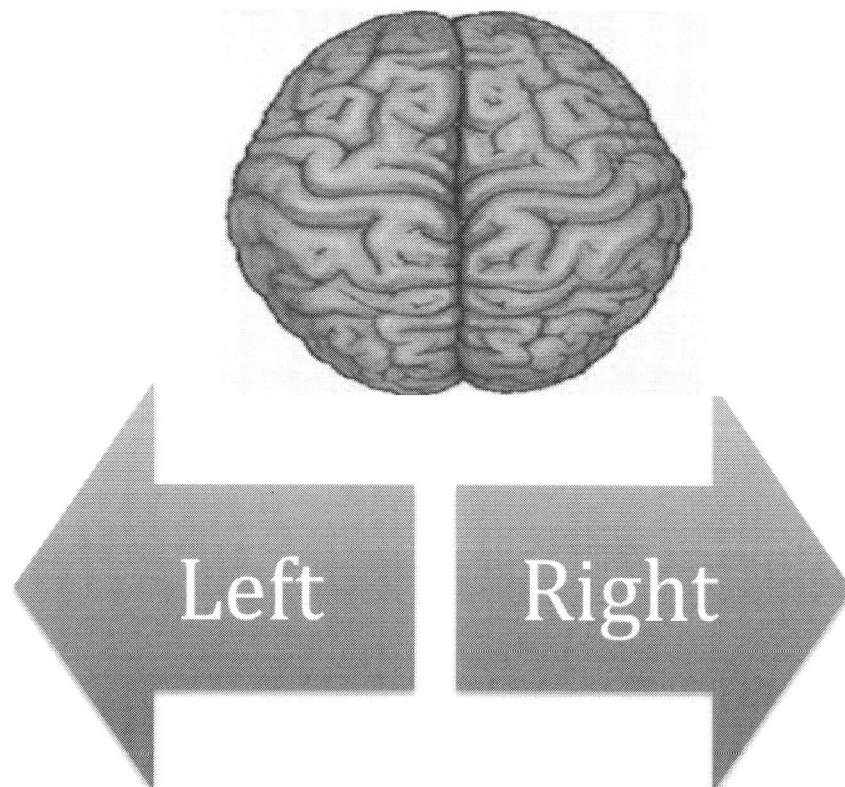

Positive Aspects;

Handles Complex Theory   Strong at Improvisation

Reads Well   Plays With Feeling

Negative Aspects;

Plays Robotically   New Material a Challenge

Can't Improvise   Can't Read

Now, if we take a look at music history, we begin to see some interesting things. For example, if we look at the same Vivaldi violin concerto from two different publishers, we find entire passages that are different.

'What's up with that?' the purist may wonder. Well, Vivaldi purposely did not write out parts for those passages. What did he put there? Chord charts, inviting the soloist to improvise something there.

Same thing with Bach's famous Chaconne in D Minor where we find an entire variation laid out in chords.

The reason we have notes in these passages today is because what some famous violinist worked out in past ages has been put there and now everyone assumes that is what was written by the composer.

The two most similar periods of music as far as musical practice goes are jazz and the baroque music of the sixteen hundreds. In a Baroque orchestra, the keyboardist served as conductor and sat next to a 'cello player. They were called the Continuo and they read entirely off of chord charts and improvised.

It seems the so-called classical musicians of this age could improvise. Mozart and Beethoven could and did improvise extensively in their public performances.

Let us go further. Bach is about the most cerebral and complex music there is, often based on some calculations that practically defy analysis. Yet, one doesn't have to understand Bach to enjoy it. The aesthetic is masterfully balanced with the intellectual aspect of the music.

Here's another example; many 'classical' musicians would be horrified if you suggested there was a similarity between Igor Stravinsky's Rite of Spring and the music of Gershwin. Yet, in an interview, Stravinsky stated that he was quite fond of American jazz and was trying to incorporate this 'primitive sound' into his music.

So it would seem the Great Divide is a recent development and quite an artificial one. I'm not going to try to go into all the reasons it came about, as that's not necessary.

All that's needed is to recognize that it's the main thing that is messing people up when they get messed up trying to learn to make music and the answer is simply a more balanced approach to learning music from the start.

Music education, especially in this country, tends to be very formatted along the Great Divide. So-called 'traditional' music lessons are not really traditional because certain elements have dropped out.

For example, music theory is considered so left-brain that many no longer see the connection between it and playing music, so it is taught as a separate subject.   There are many people who think that music theory is some lofty, ivory tower study akin to Quantum Physics but it is no such animal.

Music theory is simply the down to Earth nuts and bolts of how to play music. The trick is to decide how much theory you need to do what you want to do and apply it.

Saying you want to play music but don't want to learn any theory is like wanting to learn to drive but not wanting to know how to start a car, guide it, stop it or what side of the street to drive on.

Pop music, on the other hand, has evolved its own school of music study, something that was necessary to keep up the perception that pop music and 'classical' are very different.

How different are they? Well, consider this; the most used chords in all of western music are called the Primary Chords in 'classical' music parlance. In pop music, these *are* the Blues Chords.

'Classical' music theory actually gives a very straight forward and simple way of always finding these chords but, by calling them the Blues Chords, an element of mystery is entered in and you might think you would need a teacher who could teach them all to you.

Playing by Rote

There is a whole heck of a lot of trying to play by rote in this day and age. Playing by rote is attempting to play by pure imitation. It usually amounts to someone like a 'teacher' playing something over and over to someone else until they can play it back.

While this 'method' may work well enough for learning folk music, in attempting to learn anything longer than a page, it can only be described as a sadistic tendency.

Furthermore, there is a reason composers began to write music down. All the great folk music like Bluegrass and Gypsy would be lost if not for people like Bartok and Mel Bay who came and wrote the stuff down because, once enough of the old timers are gone, that's it, that music's gone.

One recent manifestation of rote playing was the so-called 'Suzuki Method.' Suzuki stated in the first volume of his 'method' books for violin that reading should not be taught until volume four and volume four was where you started to get concertos by Vivaldi and such.

Hence you had 'teachers' who were attempting to apply a folk music approach to learning long and complicated classical concertos.

When I first heard about this, I laughed. Then I started to run into the casualties from this and I stopped laughing.

Every student that I took over who had suffered through this 'method,' fit the same profile; they were thought to be advanced because they were in volume four. The sound they made on their instrument was a curious noise because they had no rhythm. They could not be corrected because there was nothing you could point to that they would understand.

They didn't want to learn any new music because they couldn't read music and learning a new piece meant long arduous hours of trying to imitate it.

If they didn't play the song they had 'learned' for more than a week, it was gone.

They had no rhythm because everything was done on a 'sounds like' basis. In other words there was no beat structure going on. With students who have a really good ear, sometimes this imitation can fool parents and even teachers.

So I would tell the parents, if you want to know how advanced they really are, put them in a group. They won't be able to play a single note because they won't have any idea where to put it and this was sadly true.

What a tragedy that so many individuals with perfectly good ears and probably actually quite talented were denied the joy of making music. These students were looking forward to the day when they could quit this torture and never touch the instrument again.

Pop music has its own version of rote playing going on, called TABS. TABS is short for 'Tablature' and is touted as a short-cut method for reading guitar music. The main drawback with TABS is there often is no indication of rhythm and so it, again, invites inexperienced players to play rhythm by ear. There is a version of TABS that indicates rhythm but this is usually found in books; the TABS that you get on most Internet sites do not include any notation of rhythm.

So we get the species of 'musician' who is content with learning various riffs to impress his friends and score with the chicks.

I'm also including, under this heading of 'playing by rote,' those who claim that they 'play by ear.' Now there are people who do this; instantly translate what they hear into musical notes. I haven't met one but I'm quite sure they exist. People usually cite Mozart as an example of this but he had a photographic memory so he was cheating because he was reading music even when he 'played by ear.'

The thing is, most people who claim to 'play by ear,' actually spend hours arduously pecking and hunting the notes out on their instrument until they manage to put it together, whereas someone who did read music decently *would* play it instantly.

As soon as you bring this topic up, someone pops out of the woodwork with a story about a friend or family member who can play all these songs and doesn't read a note of music.

And still the question remains, where *are* these people? They're not on the concert stage and they're not in any musical groups. You only find them at cocktail parties, I suppose, impressing their friends and scoring with the chicks.

Again, if you want to know how advanced they really are, put them in a group. They won't be able to play a single note because they won't have any idea where to put it.

Playing in a group requires an agreement on making music to a specific beat and people who play rhythm solely by ear are unable to do this.

When you read about the left-brain, right-brain theory and it says music is processed in the right side, I'm not sure what they mean by 'processed.' I think it's processed just in terms of deriving the emotional content of the sounds being made.

Really understanding what you're hearing and being able to work with that requires some sort of association with the left brain but the folks who insist on trying to play by rote seem to be stuck in the right side as far as music goes. It's a good thing these folks aren't responsible for getting a rocket to the moon; 'well, we'll just aim it up. That's where the moon is.'

The other thing about these urban legends of people who can play anything by ear is that others use this as an excuse to stop themselves from learning music.

They go 'oh I just don't have the *talent* to play music. Look at that person; he can play because he has *talent*.'

People don't say this about golf. 'Oh, look at that person. He can golf because he has talent.' No, they get some clubs and they learn some technique and then they golf.

Learning music is not that different, it's just that it's been around long enough to collect a lot of mystery and bullshit myths. The media doesn't help with this situation at all-they want to keep the idea that it's in the realm of a select few individuals.

I was appalled when an interviewer asked Eric Clapton if he practiced much and Clapton said no, he just opened his case up and threw in some meat once in a while. I'm sure Clapton was being sarcastic in the face of a stupid question; the man has obviously gotten to know the Blues Scale on a pretty intimate basis.

Everyone knows these myths, too. If you talk like I'm doing here, they'll straighten you out right away.

'Yes, you must practice six hours a day and give up your life in order to learn music. And, yes, you must have the God-given talent to play music, in which case you don't need to practice or even learn to read notes.'

I've had students who argued with me that you absolutely need to practice six hours a day, if you can imagine a teacher arguing that you don't need to practice that long. I don't want students who practice that long because, if they don't know what they're doing, they'll just iron in some real bad habits.

No one practices that long anyway. They just use that idea to stop themselves again.

'Oh, I don't have time to practice.'

'What, you don't have an hour or so a day?'

'No, I don't have six hours a day.'

'No, of course not. You're a CPA. What made you think you'd have six hours a day to practice?'

'Well, that's what it takes to play an instrument.'

'So you were planning to quit your job, change careers and practice music for six hours a day?'

'Well, no, of course not. And since I don't have six hours a day, I'm quitting.'

"You couldn't have thought of this before you bought a piano and took lessons for six months?'

Practicing *is* a waste of time-unless you have your head on very straight and do it in a very focused way.   Someone who practices two hours can get more done than another person who practices six.

That is one aim of this book; to teach you how to practice less.

Chapter Two; Why Are You Doing This, Anyway?

Now, to do this, you need a sustainable goal.

Many people, who start music lessons, either have no real goal, or they have an unsustainable goal. If you have no goal, you haven't thought the situation out very far and you're liable to never learn music.

The reason for this is, if you don't have a specific reason that you've identified, you might be doing it for some other reason altogether.

Some people take music lessons to prove that they can't be taught and their parents were wrong for making them take lessons. They go away, not being able to play music, but with the satisfaction of being right.

I had one student who kept telling me 'don't try to teach me 'The Bear Climbed Over The Mountain!'

I assured him I wouldn't dream of it, but it turned out he was mad because his brother got the music lessons and he didn't and *he* had the great ear. So all he wanted to prove was he had a great ear and didn't need music lessons, so he didn't learn anything, of course.

Some people, on the other hand, have unsustainable goals. Here's an example of an unsustainable goal;

A student wanted to sound like Elton John. He got the sheet music for Elton John's songs and worked hard to learn them and said it didn't sound like Elton John.

I told him that was because what was on the sheet music wasn't what Elton John did. I told him, if he wanted to sound like Elton John, he would have to learn chords really well and also learn how to improvise.

Well, this was too much for him. The real problem was that he was sort of a left-sided musician and he needed to be more right-sided. This can be done, actually and I'll explain this later on but he wasn't prepared to do anything like this.

Another guy only wanted to play only Beethoven. The only problem here was his wanting to bypass a few levels of music theory to get to Ludwig faster. As a consequence, he never played exactly what Beethoven wrote, so it wasn't Beethoven.

As a teacher, you feel obliged to do something since they're paying you, so you offer some corrections and they just end up resenting you. You're supposed to sit there and tell them how remarkable they are, playing Beethoven mostly by ear.

Well, it was true that I never heard anything quite like it.

Now, between the time I took lessons and the time I started to teach, the scene had changed rather drastically.

When I was a pup, if you took music lessons that meant you wanted to go to music school and become a professional musician.

By the time I started teaching, students who planned to go on to music school had become much more rare and a new breed of student had taken their place.

I remember one time some parents explained to me that their kids were not going to be musicians, (they were going to be lawyers or gynecologists) and they were taking music lessons for 'enrichment,' for lack of a better term. They supposed that I would be sorely discouraged over this but I had been to music school and it wasn't something that I recommended to anyone but the stoutest of spirits.

As I mulled over this 'enrichment' idea I saw, that to impart greater value to the person, they would still have to acquire a skill.

So, in a way, it wasn't much different; they would still have to learn to play music it's just that they wouldn't be going to music school.

So it was essentially the same thing, without the five hours of practicing a day and the Nazi teacher who beat them on their wrists with his baton and screamed at them.

I could live with that.

I had already seen the research on Facebook and knew that mean teachers didn't live as long.

Once I made this decision, there was only one rule I needed to be strict about and that was, students with bad attitudes must go.

After a time, I had a schedule made up of mostly students who were pleasant to teach.

One thing I began to notice was that a lot of these students got quite good. They also tended to develop a genuine enjoyment of music and could play just about anything you put in front of them.

My point here is that playing music well and *correctly* is its own reward, even if the pieces you play are rather simple.

I'm offering this as a sustainable goal for you, in the beginning; to be able to play music well and *correctly*, even if the pieces are rather simple.

In the first place, this goal aligns you with the greatest musicians on the planet. Do you suppose that a great musician such as Arthur Rubenstein had a goal like 'I'm going to become world famous and wealthy, playing this instrument I don't like and music I can't stand?'

By having a goal to enjoy making music, you are sharing at least a sub-product with every great musician everywhere. Humans enjoy accomplishing something and accomplishing playing music has the added reward of the music itself.

Ah, but you may say, 'I have much greater aspirations for myself with regards to learning music.' Fine. This is not to say you can't set a different goal or a larger one, once you have achieved this first one.

Here's the thing; if you cannot play simple music well and *correctly*, you will never master more complicated music. The most complex musical works are made from the same basics that go into the simplest music.

If there's music you can't play it's not because it's too hard or you're too dumb or because you need to learn a secret Masonic hand shake or offer your virginity up to Beelzebub. It's because some very basic music skill is out and has probably been out since day one of your music lessons.

On the other hand, if you can play simple music well and correctly, there's no reason you can't tackle more difficult stuff.

Chapter Three; Plays Well With Others.

By now you've probably noticed that I've emphasized playing *correctly,* as opposed to 'playing around.' So how do you know if you are playing correctly?

Well, I've offered the test of playing with a group or another musician as one sure test.

Try playing with another musician. If you have trouble in this regard it's either the other musician or you. Try playing with someone else or a group. If the trouble persists, it's you.

The reason for this phenomenon is that good musicians play with an agreed upon beat. In other words, they deliberately set the speed of the beat they are going to play with and use their rhythm skills to play the rhythm in accordance with the speed of that beat or 'tempo' as it's called.

They can change the speed of the beat, making it faster or slower, if they so choose, and can still play their parts correctly.

Someone who has not learned to work with a beat has fallen into the trap of trying to play rhythm by ear and often will not be able to adjust the tempo he has learned his music with.

This goes even further because everything the person plays can be without a beat and be lifeless and unexpressive because it's not really music. Despite this person's argument that learning 'too much' theory will kill the feeling of the music he thinks he is imparting, the opposite is true because rhythm and expression are integral.

Now why get this far to discover you've developed a very bad habit that needs to be corrected and have to go back and do it right?

Most people have a very hard time with this as no one likes to go back to square one, especially when they think they've gotten to be pretty advanced.

Correcting this in students needs to be done very gently and gradually, if they are to be recovered at all.

Having said all this, it makes sense that one's music study should begin with rhythm.

A metronome is an essential tool to have, in the beginning. A metronome is a device that is either wind-up or electric and it gives you a beat to work with.

The metronome can be set to give you different speeds of beat. The speeds or tempos range from slow (around 40 beats a minute,) to fast, (around 250 beats a minute.) The wind-up metronome can be set to different speeds by moving the little metal bar up or down on the pendulum, which is the thin metal strip that moves back and forth as it ticks.

The electric metronome can be set to different tempos by two buttons, (usually an up or down arrow.) Many metronomes also have Italian words that indicate the different tempos but you don't have to worry about these as all you'll be doing, in the beginning, is setting the tempo to a speed that seems comfortable to practice your rhythms with. In the beginning, I recommend a tempo anywhere from 70 to 90.

You use the metronome at the very beginning of your studies to practice your rhythm drills.

In practicing your rhythm drills, first clap or tap the rhythms out. When you are proficient at this, play the rhythms on your instrument in a simple fashion.

For example, on the piano, the rhythms could be done using a single key. On a string instrument such as a guitar or violin, they could be played on an open string.

It is important to use the metronome and play the same rhythm over several times, using different tempos. The final stage in this is to turn off the metronome and count out a tempo to use. Do this several times on the same rhythm with different tempos as well. This will be explained in greater detail in the next chapter.

Most music students own a metronome that they never use and they hate it. This is because no one ever showed them the correct way to use one. They usually wait until it becomes apparent that there is rhythm or tempo problems in some piece that they are working on and then they put the metronome on at the tempo they think they are playing at.

At this stage, it is too late. They have not been aware of using any particular beat in their music up to this point and so they cannot play with the metronome at all. They get frustrated and hide the metronome away in their piano bench and never use it again.

Therefore, your first action in learning to play music is the next chapter, where you will learn all the rhythm basics and find drills to practice in the ways I have outlined above.

It's easy and it's fun and, hey, maybe you'll decide to play the drums instead

Chapter Four; Rhythm; We'll Make A Drummer Out Of You Yet.

There's nothing more pathetic than a drummer who can't keep a steady beat, unless it's an instrumentalist or a singer. Singers are reputedly the worst.

I once had a string quartet that played weddings and we had a gig with a singer who was someone's mother-in-law. We were going to play 'The Wedding Song' with her and I had made an arrangement based exactly on the sheet music.

We were rehearsing in the church the morning of the wedding and invited her to come on down and practice with us. She did not. She went out and bought candles.

So we made the mistake of trying to wing it with a singer we knew nothing about. What could go wrong?

Well, she had no musical training and learned by listening to recordings. Needless to say, we were together with her for about a second and she went off ahead of us, winging along in her own right-sided way.

This chapter is also for the would-be songwriter or composer. Many people have great ideas in their heads but can't get them down on paper or get them across in any other way.

How is this solved? With what's right here in this chapter. So let's begin.

We'll start with the needed definitions for this chapter on rhythm.

First is the **time signature**. It looks like this;

4

4

The time Signature is two numbers that appear at the very beginning of a piece of music. The top number tells you how many beats are in each **measure**.

What's a **measure**?

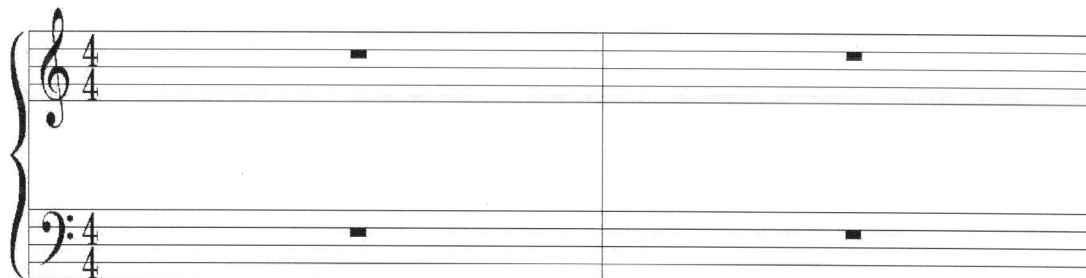

See the line on the very far right side? That's a **measure line** and every four beats there will be another **measure line** and these divide the music up into **measures**.

If the top number of the **time signature** were a three, then the **measure lines** would come every three beats. The top number can, theoretically be anything but it is typically 2, 3 or 4. 'Four four' is so common that it is often referred to as **common time** and, instead of the two fours, you will just see a large letter **C**.

The **beat** is a steady pulse that governs the speed or **tempo** of the music. The **tempo** can be fast or slow or anything in between. The **tempo** is found at the top of the music like this;

Quickly

Tempo has often been indicated by Italian words. A number can also indicate **tempo**, which is a metronome speed. The **tempo** and the **time signature** are not synonymous.

Next, we'll be getting familiar with the different types of notes. I'll show you the note; give its name and also the **counting.**

An important note about **counting; counting** is one of those basic tools that you should master and use. **Counting** will clear up any musical difficulty immediately.

The way you count is to count the beats in each **measure** of a piece. If the piece has four beats in a **measure**, you **count** to four and, if it has three beats in a **measure**, you **count** to three. You can **count** out loud or in your **head**.

You **count** in a specific **tempo** that you decide. You can quickly acquire this skill of counting by putting metronome on at any speed and counting along with it. Notes have specific durations or lengths determined by how many **beats** or **counts** they get. If a note gets two **counts** or **beats**, it is held to a count of two.

For those notes where there is more than one note on a single **beat**, additional syllables are added to the **count** to indicate the additional notes. The syllables have no significance and are neutral.

I want to add one more thing, before we introduce the various notes, and that is that the note durations were decided in the simplest way possible; they're fractional.

If you took the largest note and began to divide it up like a pizza, in other words, by half, quarters, eights and so on, you would get the same scheme used to decide the different note durations. In fact the notes are named after these fractions.

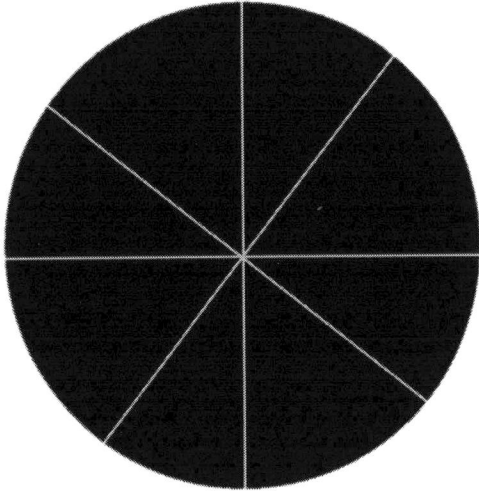

After each note, we will show the equivalent 'rest,' which gets the same number of beats or counting but you don't play it.

So let us begin with the largest note, which is called the whole note. (Note the resemblance to a whole pizza.)

As you can see, the whole note is just a circle or 'head.' You can see, as well, that the Whole note gets four counts or beats. You hold this note while you count to four.

Here's the whole rest;

Next comes, you guessed it, the **half note**. Yes, we've cut the **whole note** in half and the **half note** gets two **counts**.

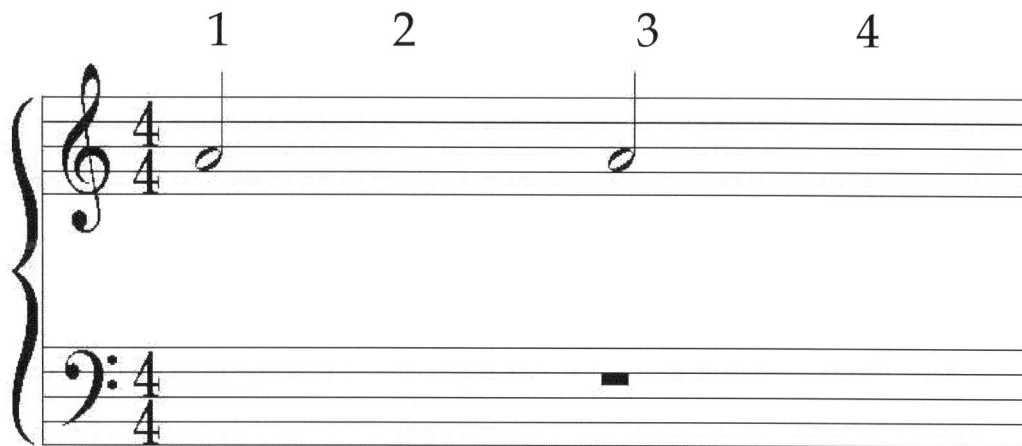

The **half rest** looks like this;

Moving right along, we next have the **quarter note**. Last time I checked, half of two was one, and that's how many beats the **quarter note** gets.

In 'four four' time, quarter notes are synonymous with the beat.

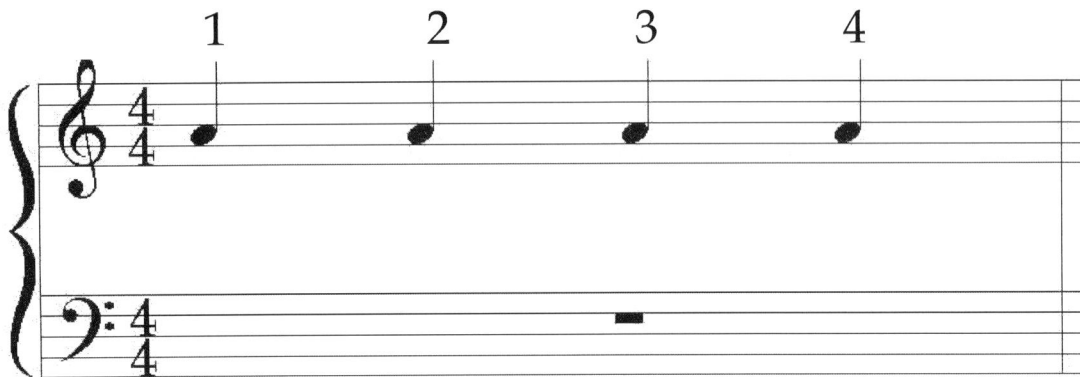

This is the **quarter rest;**

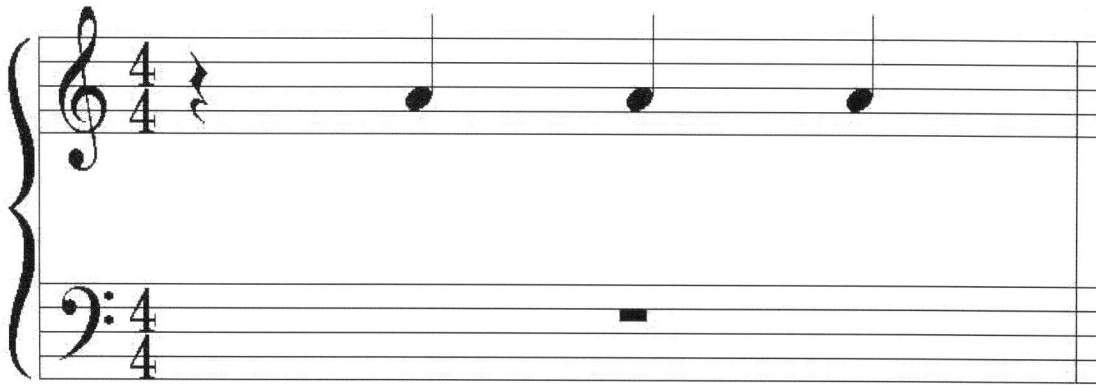

Now is as good a time as any to identify the parts of a note. The circular part is the **head** and this is the most important part for reading the note. We'll cover this in more detail in the chapter on reading. The line is called the **stem**.

Now the **eighth note**, in addition to having a **head** and a **stem**, also has a **flag**.

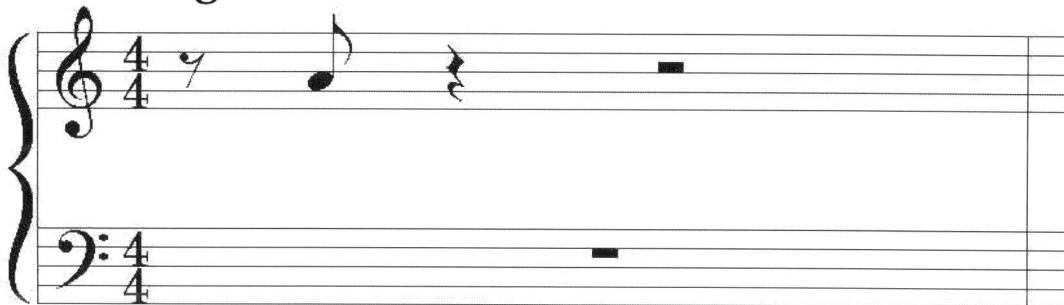

The hangy-down part is the flag, so the **eighth note** has one **flag**. The **eighth note** is half a beat so, to make life simpler, they are often paired two on a beat, and you just play them twice as fast as **quarter notes**. The little hook jobby in front of this one is the **eight rest**.

When they are paired, their flags are hooked together or barred so they look like this;

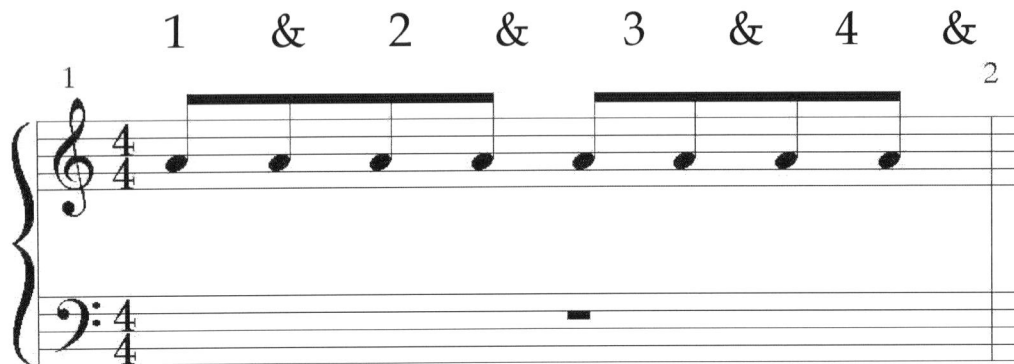

Here is where you begin to use the neutral syllables since there are two notes in each **count,** so you get the **count** followed by an 'and.' You will have to **count** twice as fast to get both the number and the 'and' in and keep the same beat.

Eighth rests are never **'barred.'**

Then comes the **sixteenth note** with two **flags;**

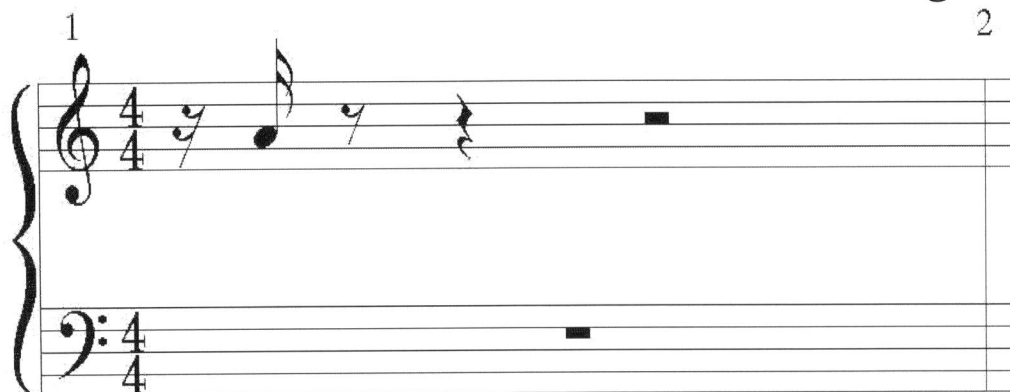

Again, the double hooked job in front is its rest.

This note is a quarter of a beat and they are frequently **'barred'** together, four of them making a single beat;

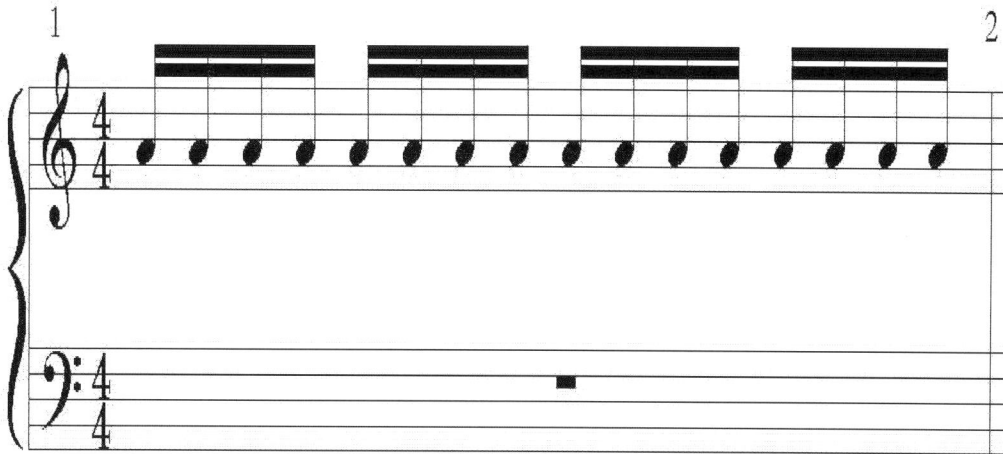

1 e & a   2 e & a   3 e & a   4 e & a

Note the counting; four syllables, a syllable for each note. They are played four on a beat.

The **sixteenth rest** is also never '**barred**.'

By now, you should get the idea. This dividing up of the pizza or whole note is carried on to **32nd** notes, which get three flags and are eight on a beat, as are the rests and finally to **64th** notes, getting four flags and being 16 on a beat.

The syllable method of **counting,** in my opinion, breaks down with the **32nd** notes as it just becomes too unwieldy to be of practical use.

This should not discourage you in regards to these last two note types as it's just a matter of being able to hear notes twice as fast each time you go from a larger to the next smaller.

The **counting** should instill this ability in you, if you use it regularly and so you can gauge the 32nds by making them twice as fast as the **sixteenths**.

Additionally, **32nds** and **64**[th] show up mainly in slower tempos as a fast beat makes them impractical for the large part.

This next section contains practical drills you can use to apply the information I've given above. For optimum results, print out the pages with the drills and write in the counting on the line below each drill, using the **counting** I've given you for each type of note or rest.

Then use your **metronome** to clap the rhythm or tap it on a table. Set your metronome to a comfortable speed. I recommend seventy to eighty beats per minute to start with for the first ones and then a bit slower for the ones that have **sixteenth notes**. Again, for optimum results, play each exercise several times using different speeds or **tempos**.

Then you will want to play the drill without the metronome, using the counting. Remember that, when you do this, it is very important that *you* set the **tempo** and count in that **tempo**.

A good way to do this is to count off a **preparatory measure** before you start the drill. You simply **count** off an empty **measure.** If the top number in your **time signature** indicates four beats in a measure, you simply **count** to four and start. If the top number indicates three beats in a **measure**, you count to three and so on.

The speed in which you count off in the **preparatory measure** sets your **tempo,** and then you stick with that speed or **tempo** in the playing of that particular song or musical piece.

This action of you deliberately picking a **tempo** to play in is one of the most important musical skills you need to have and you're fairly lost without it.

You can also follow the link below to listen to the drills online.

Rhythm Drills

Unless otherwise indicated, all Rhythm Drills in this book are in **'four four time.'**

Rhythm Drill 1A;

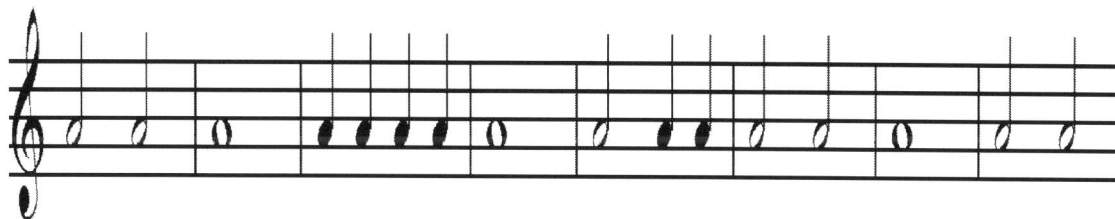

Rhythm Drill 2A;

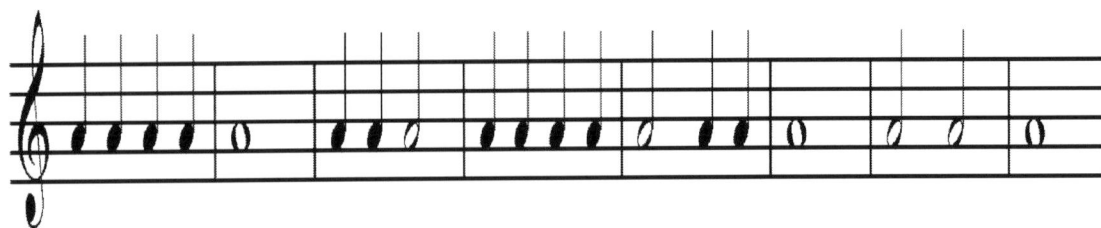

Rhythm Drill 3A;

Rhythm Drill 4A

Rhythm Drill 5A;

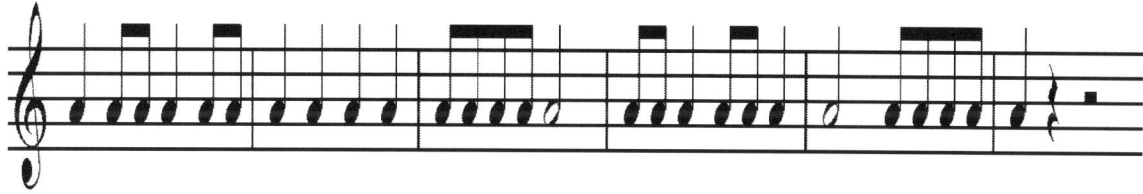

Rhythm Drill 6A;

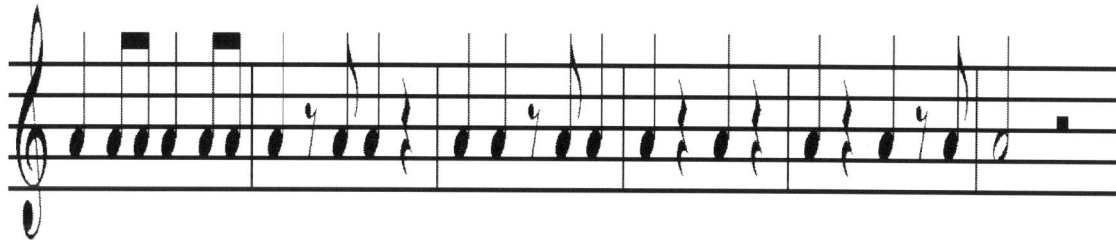

Rhythm Drill 7A;

Rhythm Drill 8A;

Rhythm Drill 9A;

A curved line connecting two note that are the same pitch (same line or space) is called a **tie**. The tie makes them into one note that is **counted** as the total count of both notes.

Rhythm Drill 10A;

You often see a note with a **dot** after it. The **dot rule** is that the **dot** adds half more to the note, thus a **half note** with a **dot** gets three beats and a quarter note with a **dot** gets one and a half beats.

Here is how a **dotted quarter note** would be counted;

1 2 & 3 4

Rhythm Drill 11A;

Rhythm Drill 12A;

A three, placed over 3 notes, turns the notes into a **triplet.** The **triplet** is a different amount of **beats**, depending on what kind of notes become **triplets**. For example, a **quarter note triplet** is two beats but an **eighth note triplet** is one beat. The **eight-note triplet** is the most common, and is counted like this;

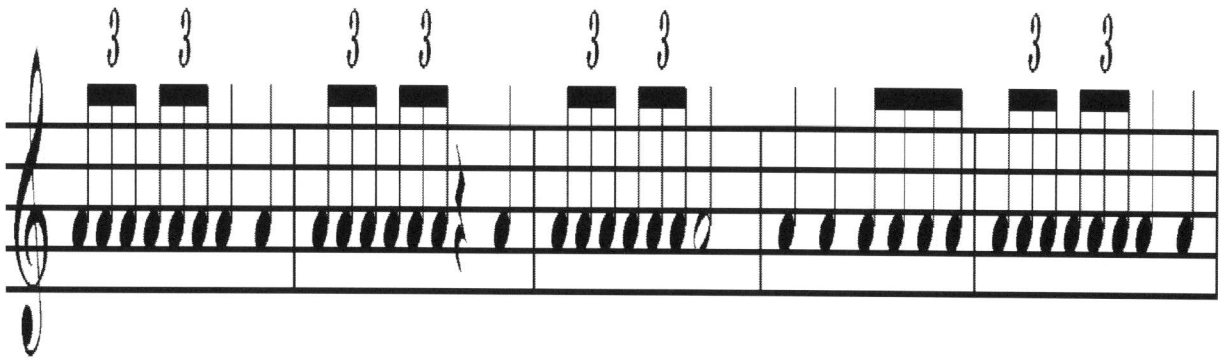

In summary, Rhythm should be the first skill that you master, with special attention to **counting** and learning to set the **tempo**.

Now you will not count every time you play a piece of music. The optimum time to employ counting is the *first few times you play through a new piece.*

This enables you to get the **rhythm** straight from the start. From there you should have established a good sense of the **beat**.

Remember to get into a habit of establishing the **beat** or **tempo** *every time you start playing* by counting a **preparatory measure**, either out loud or in your head.

Go to www.dizzyobriansnewmusic.com/rhythm-drills, to listen to these rhythm drills online.

Chapter Five; To Read Or Not To Read.

The next step is, of course, learning about the notes in music. Now you may or may not want or need to learn to read music.

As I think I've indicated, people in a pop band usually do not read off of a music score. They know the music theory that pertains to improvising which is chord theory, scales and key signatures.

Knowing about how musical notes are written, however, makes learning this theory *way easier*.

Keep in mind that, knowing about how music is written, and actually reading music are two different things. I will endeavor to explain this as I go.

Now, in the Rhythm drills in the last chapter, you've been looking at notes that were placed on a series of five lines and four spaces called a **staff**.

Let's take a closer look at this and we'll review some previous terms as we go.

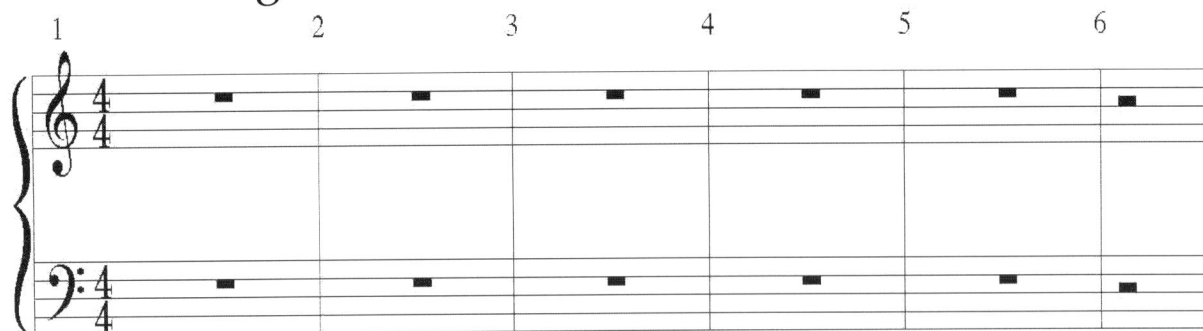

What you see here are two **staffs** linked together with a 'brace.' This arrangement is used for keyboard instruments like the piano. Most other instruments use only one **staff**.

As you can see, each **staff** has five lines and, in between the lines are four spaces.

I think we mentioned that the circular part of a note is called the **'head,'** the line is called a **'stem,'** and some notes have a **'flag.'**

Let's put a note on this staff now.

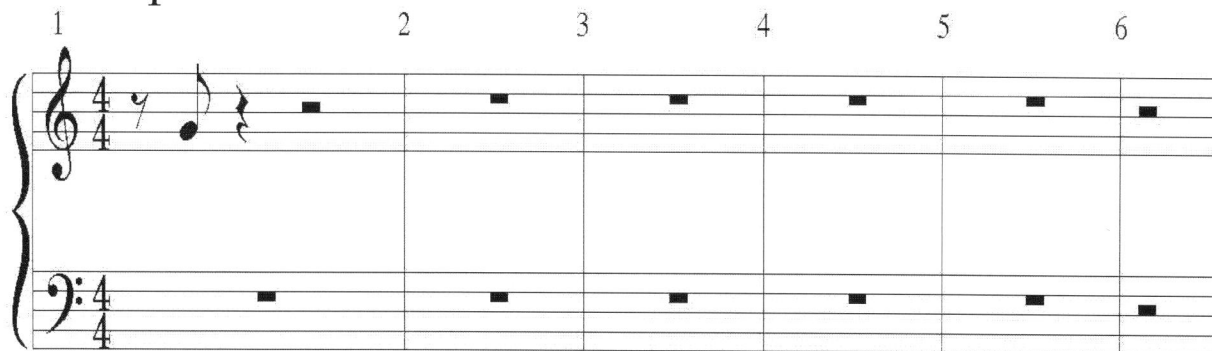

There, we put an **eighth note** on the top **staff**. If you look at the **'head'** of the note, you see that a line runs right through it, so this note is on a line, in fact, it's on the second line of the top **staff**.

The **head** of the note is what's important in terms of identifying the note. The **stem** and the **flag** show it's an **eighth note** and they can go up or down but, what matters, is what line or space the **head** of the note is on.

Let's put a different note on the **staff** now.

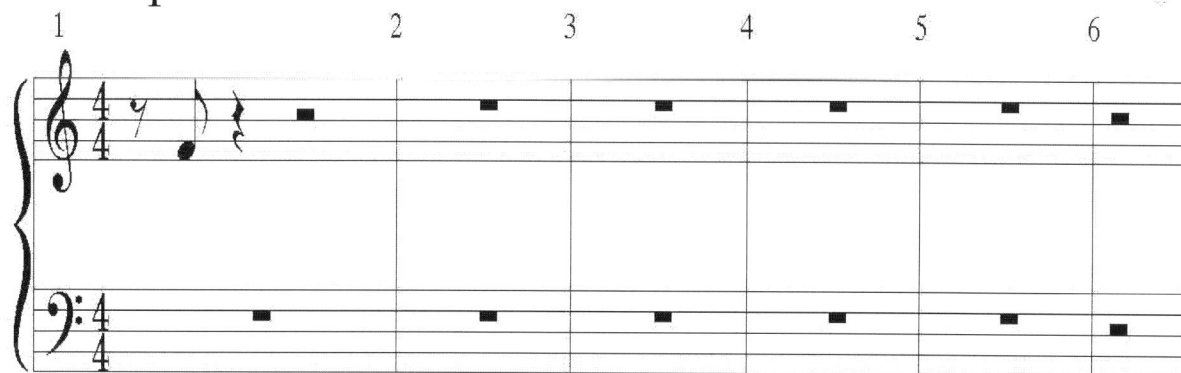

Now, as you can see, the **head** of this note is in a space, the first space in the top **staff.**

So how *do* you identify musical notes? With the **musical alphabet**, of course. The **musical alphabet** is simply the first seven letters of the alphabet. *Bet* you didn't think it was that simple.

It goes; **a b c d e f g**, and then repeats from **a** again (and again and again.) each line and space is assigned a letter, depending on the '**clef**' that is used.

That funky looking thing in the top **staff**, just in front of the **time signature**, is called a '**g' clef** or '**treble clef.'**

It's called a '**g' clef** because it looks something like the letter **G** and it curves around the second line of a **staff** showing that this line is **G.**

So, if that line is **G**, that makes the first line **E** and, going from there, line to space and space to line, it goes **E F G A B C D E F**. The note we put on the line above is **G**, in this case, and the note we put in the space is **F**.

Therefore, the lines are **E G B D F**, and the spaces are; **F A C E**.

For quick reference, use the mnemonic '**Every Good Bird Does Fly**,' for the lines and, gee, if only the spaces spelled a word or something, *that* would make it easy to remember.

The clef in the bottom staff is called the '**bass clef**' or '**f' clef**, because it looks something like the letter **f**, and the line that passes between the two dots is **F**. Repeating the same process of assigning letters to every space and line, then the lines work out to being **G B D F A** and the spaces become **A C E G**.

You can work out your own mnemonic for all this but suggested ones are; **Great Big Dogs Fight Animals**, for the lines and **All Cars Eat Gas**, for the spaces.

Yes, you can go off of the **staff** and it looks like this;

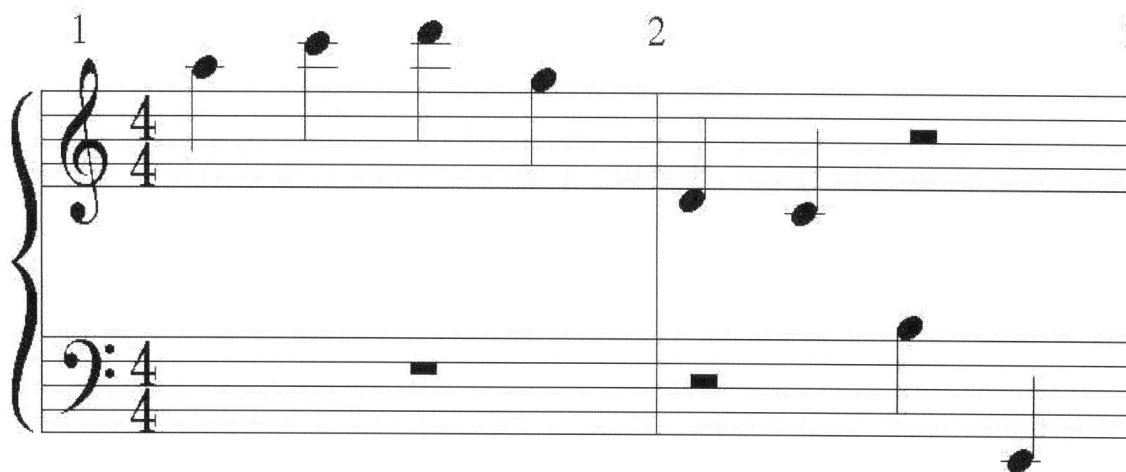

It's just a matter of adding more lines and spaces. The lines are much smaller is all and they are called **ledger lines**. It's the same principle though; every space and line is a note.

To figure them out, just go forwards in the alphabet when going higher and backwards, when going lower.

For greater speed in reading **ledger lines**, just memorize certain ones to use as landmarks. For example, two lines above the **treble staff** is 'C.'

Orientation

Proper orientation is essential for ease and speed in reading musical notes.

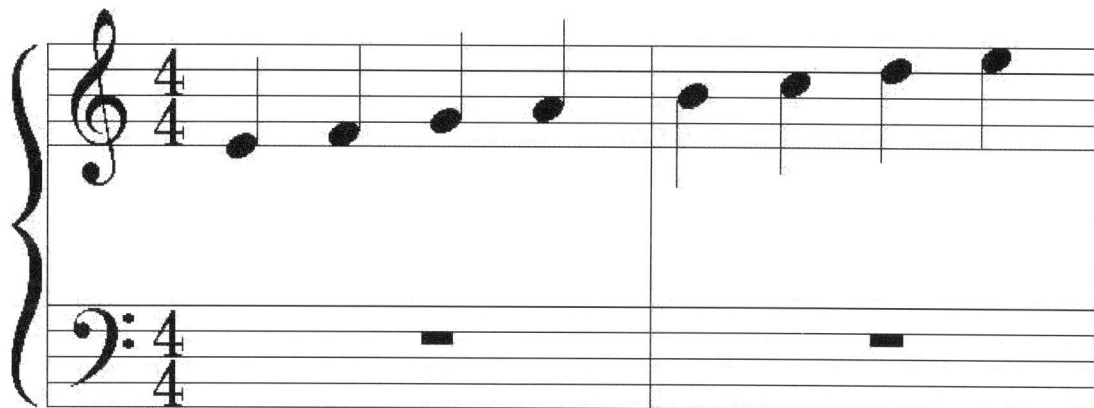

Looking at the example above, we can see that there is a note in every consecutive line and space, reading from left to right.

These notes are going **up** in a **stepwise** fashion. In other words, one note going up to the very next note. The notes are getting progressively higher up on the staff and each line note is followed by the very next space note and so on.

This would follow the Musical Alphabet in order but starting with E. So it would go; **E, F, G, A, B, C, D, E. Stepwise** always goes in order of the alphabet, no matter what letter you start on and, when you get to G, you always start again with A.

You would also need to know up and down on your instrument. For example, on a keyboard, up is to the right so going up **stepwise** on a piano would mean going from one white key to the very next white key to the right.

This, of course is the same series of notes, only going down. All the information about stepwise movement from before applies but the notes are going down.

The Alphabet progresses backwards, in this case; **E D C B A G F E**.

This note-by-note progression is also referred to as a **scale**, which is one of the only two patterns used in music.

Why is this information important? The theory information I give in this book is only important in so far as it makes playing *easier*.

So here's how this makes playing easier.

When reading music becomes painful to a person and they give it up, it's because they are over-thinking the process.

How are they over-thinking it? By thinking they have to stop and find the name of every note as they go.

How can this over-think be avoided? By breaking the notes down into simple patterns when ever possible and using those instead,

A **scale** is about the simplest pattern in music there is. Note by note either up or down.

So, if you recognize a **scale** pattern in your music that goes up, you simply find the starting note and then play each white key to the right until you run out of notes (if you're playing keyboards.)

If you're playing a string instrument, like the guitar, you just keep putting down fingers and moving to the next higher string.

Similarly, if the **scale** goes down, you just keep playing each white key to the left or, on a string instrument, take fingers off and move to the next lower string.

Since **scales** are one of the only two patterns in music, you constantly run across **scales** in music. You find **scales** in all lengths, short and long, but they all go up or down **stepwise.**

Recognizing Intervals

Intervals in music are another very simple but highly usable concept. The term **interval** means the distance between any two notes and it is expressed with numbers.

The smallest interval is the **second** or **step**, and we have examined this one already in the **scale**. The second is when you go up or down to the very next note and, on the page it is one note on a line and the next in the very next space or visa versa.

Obviously you can move up or down and skip some notes; hence our next **interval** is the **third**.

In counting **intervals,** you start on one note and count it as one, you count all lines and spaces between it and the other note and you count the other note. In the examples above you get three for each.

Another way to look at it is you are counting the letters between two notes inclusively.

If the notes come one after the other, as in the examples above, they are called **melodic intervals.**

They can also occur on the same stem, in which instance they are played simultaneously. These are called **harmonic intervals**.

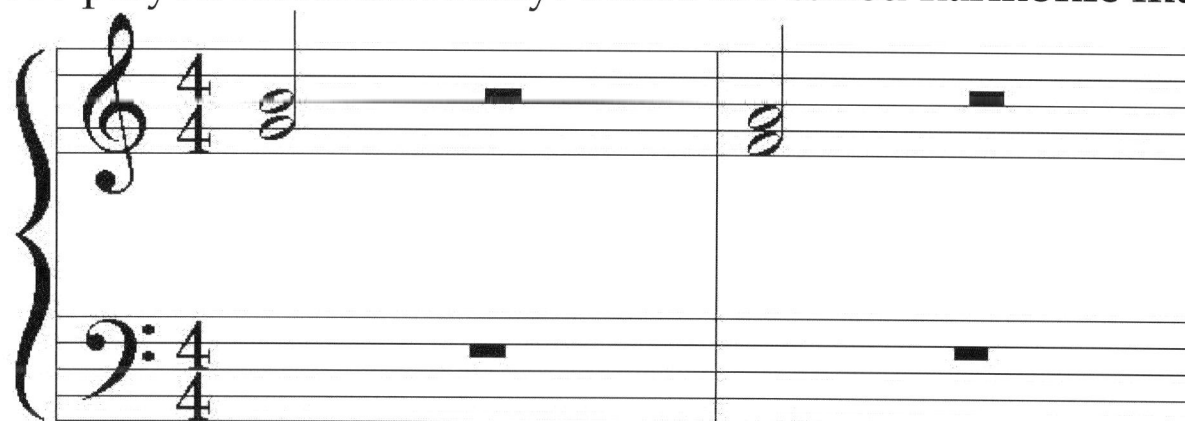

    Intervals generally go up to the 8th, which is also called an **octave**, but they can go larger.

    With a little experience, **intervals** are easy to spot. For one thing, the even numbers are on different things, i.e. one note on a line, the other on a space, while the odd numbers are on the same thing, i.e. both on lines or both on spaces.

    This is the first thing you want to spot; is it odd or even? Then you can kind of eyeball it by its size. Soon you will be able to see what the **interval** is without having to count the lines and spaces.

This will greatly increase your speed and ease of reading because you will be able to see which direction the notes are going (up or down) and if they are stepping or skipping. You will be able to tell right away how large the skip is.

You should be able to play pretty long passages in this way, only needing to find your starting note.

To sum up this part, rather than trying to read notes by identifying every note as you go and finding it on your instrument, read more by following the up and down movements of the notes and if they are skipping or going **stepwise**.

Use the mnemonics for quick reference and drill note recognition separately with musical flashcards until note recognition is quick and doesn't require a lot of thought.

Chapter Six; Sharps and Flats

So we've talked about the **musical alphabet.** Now, on a keyboard, these letters are the white keys.

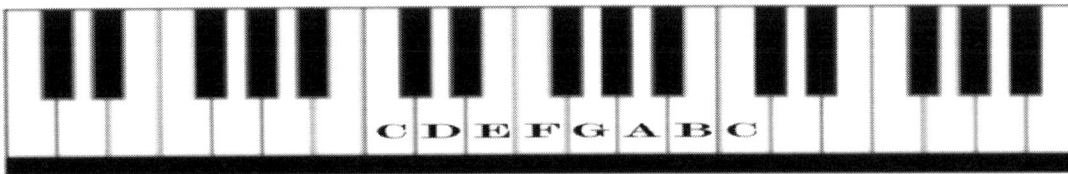

C D E F G A B C

We've also talked about how going from one letter to the next is called a **step**.

Well, the next thing to know is there are two sizes of steps; the **whole step** and the **half step**.

As you've no doubt noticed, there are black keys in between many of the white keys.

The basic definition of a **half step** is the closest key or note that you can go to. So most of the white keys are not the closest key or note you can go to because they have a black key in between.

So going from one letter to the next with a black key in the middle is a **whole step** because it's two **half steps.**

You can also notice, however, there are two sets of white keys that have no black key in the middle; the **E&F** and the **B&C**. These white keys are **half steps.**

So what is all this business of Half Steps about? Well, these are your **sharps** and **flats.**

A **sharp** is the closest note or **half step** to the right or *higher*. The **sharp** is placed directly to the left of the note that is to be sharped on the same line or space.

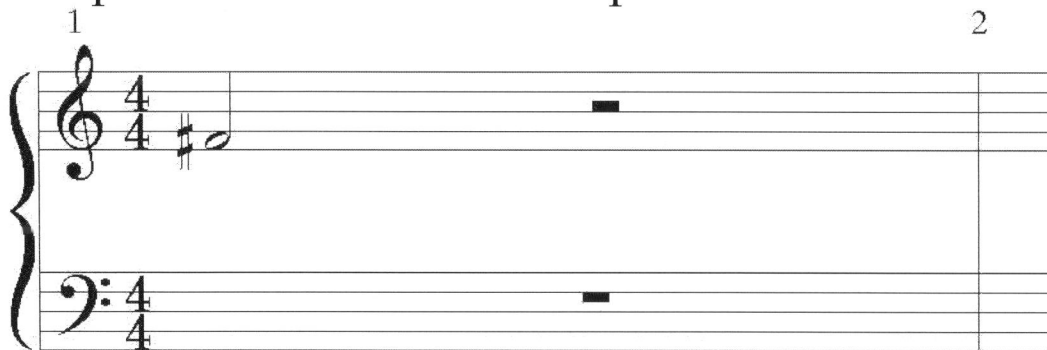

If the example above was in **treble clef**, the note would be an '**F sharp'**. It would be played by playing the black key to the right of the white key '**F'** on the picture of the keyboard above.

A **flat** is the closest note or **half step** to the left or *lower*. The **flat** is placed directly to the left of the note that is to be flatted on the same line or space.

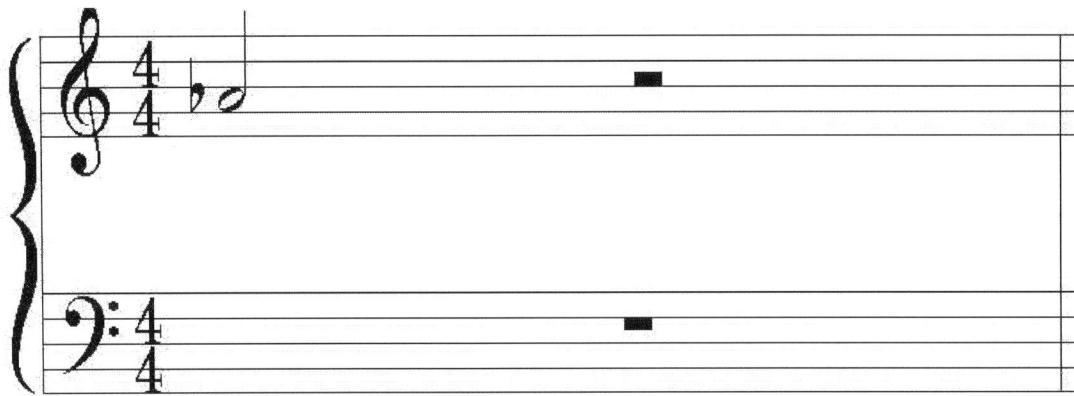

This **A** would now be an **A flat** and played by playing the closest black key to the left of the white key A in the picture of the keyboard above.

The white keys are called **naturals**.

The **natural** sign is not really needed unless it's to cancel a **sharp** or a **flat**. Here's how that works;

The **sharp**, **flat** or **natural** are called **accidentals** when placed before a note in any given measure. **Accidentals** are good for the measure meaning, if the same note occurs in that **measure**, the **accidental** still holds. In the example above, the second **A** would still be **flat** because it's in the same **measure**, so a **natural** sign is needed, if the second **A** is to be a **natural**. In a subsequent measure that had an **A** in it, the **flat** would no longer be in effect.

As you also may have noticed, the notes on the keyboard form a **scale**. This **scale** is called the **C scale** because it starts on **C**.

The **C** scale is the only scale that is all **naturals** and no **sharps** or **flats**. This is important and the **C scale** is one of the first things you should learn on any instrument because, if you don't know where the **naturals** are, **sharps** and **flats** will confuse the heck out of you.

Also very important to take note of the fact that the **C scale** has its own **half steps** between the **E** and the **F** and the **B** and the **C**.

So, if you're looking for **B sharp**, now where do you suppose it will be found?

Chapter Seven; Key Signatures and Scales

If you said that the '**C**' was the **B sharp**, move to the head of the class. Those are, after all, one of the sets of white key **half steps**.

This is a good juncture to go over the concept of **key** or **tonality**. Most all Western (hemisphere) music operates on the illusion that one note or key is stronger than the rest and the music doesn't sound 'done,' until that note is reached.

People respond to this without any music lessons what so ever.

It's a very simple thing, initially; the first note of any scale operates as the **key** or **tonality**.

Now I'm bringing this up because **sharps** and **flats** have been mainly and traditionally used to shift or change the **key** or **tonality** to a different note. Here's how *that* works;

In the previous section I explained how **accidentals** work. There is another way that **sharps** and **flats** can be applied and that is the **key signature**.

A certain number of **sharps** or **flats** are placed at the very beginning of the music, just before the **time signature.**

They are put on specific lines or spaces, indicating that the notes of those lines or spaces are sharped or flatted throughout the music.

Due to the shift in the arrangement of **whole steps** and **half steps** that this creates, a new **key** or **tonality** is created.

Now there is a lot of information about the order that the **sharps** or **flats** come in and what goes on with the order of the **whole steps** and the **half steps** but I am going to give you the short method of identifying the key right now, because that's what you really want to know in playing; what **key** you're in and what **sharps** or **flats** to apply.

Many is the time I have sat in with a band on stage with no rehearsal and they will ask me, 'can I do this or can I do that?' and I just say, 'tell me the **key** and some of the chords and I'll be fine.'

Usually there's one member who can tell me this information and then we're good.

So here's the short method for identifying what key a piece of music is in. For **keys** that have **sharps**, go to the last **sharp** and go up one letter (a half step) and that will be the name of the Key. For example, in the case of four **sharps**;

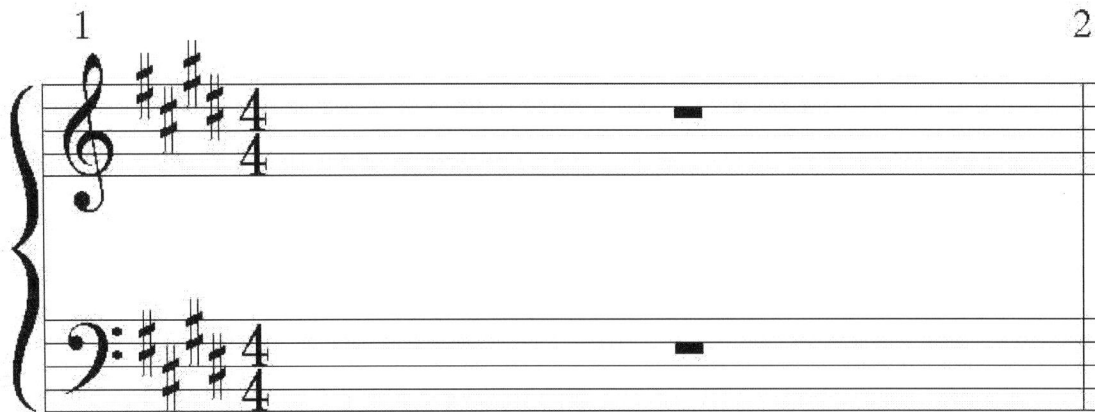

The four **sharps** here are **F C G** and **D**, in that order. The last **sharp** is **D**, so going up a letter, you get **E** as the name of the **key**.

For **keys** that have **flats**, back up one **flat** from the last **flat** and that will give you the name of the **key**. For example, five **flats**;

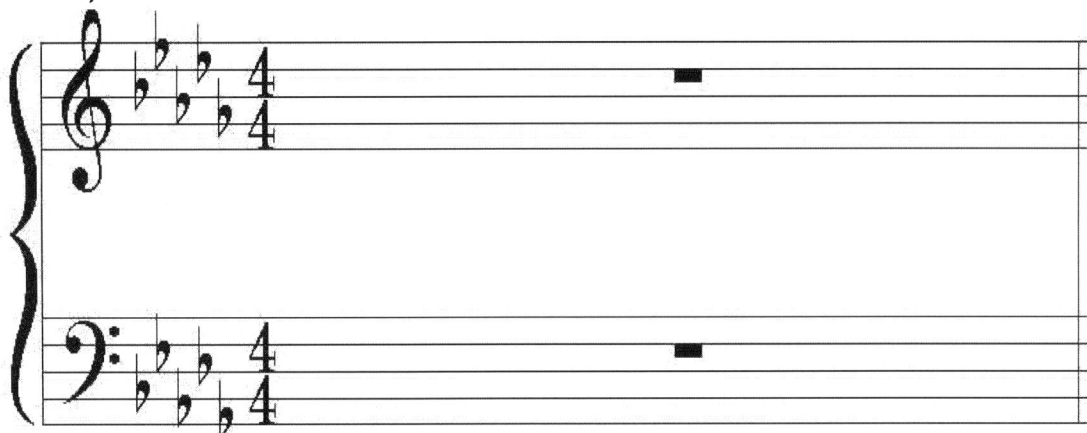

The five **flats** here are **B E A D** and **G,** in that order, so the last one is **G** and, backing up to the one before that gives you the key of **D flat**.

This short method does not work on **C Major** since its **key signature** has *no* **sharps** or **flats**. It also doesn't work for **F Major** because this **key** has only one **flat** so there is no **flat** to back up to.

Every **key** has a **scale** that begins on the note that that **key** is named after and it uses whatever **sharps** or **flats** are in the **key signature**. Traditional **scales** span at least an **octave** or eight notes.

For example, the **scale** of **E Major** would go from **E** and the **F, C G** and **D** would be sharped. The **scale** of **D flat** major would start on **D flat** and the **B, E A** and **D** would be flatted.

All major **scales** have the same pattern of **whole steps** and **half steps**, which is they have **half steps** between the third and fourth notes and the seventh and eighth notes, the rest being **whole steps**.

It is certainly worthwhile to learn and practice the different **scales**, applying your **rhythm** skills to them.

Relative Minor Scales

Every **major scale** has a **relative minor scale** that goes with it. It is called the **relative minor** because it uses the same **key signature;** only the **scale** begins on a different note.

To find a **major scale's relative minor**, go down three **half steps** or go up to the sixth note of the **major scale.**

For example, the **relative minor** for **C Major** is 'a' minor.

There are three versions or forms of the **minor scale**.

The first is called **natural minor** and it makes no change in the notes from what is in the **key signature**.

The second one is called the **melodic minor** and it raises the sixth and seventh notes of the **scale** each a **half step** on the way up but reverts to the **key signature** on the way down.

The third one is the most used one and it is called the **harmonic minor** and it raises the seventh note a **half step** both up and down.

There are other types of scales such as the **pentatonic scale** and the **modes**, which will be defined later in the book.

Chapter Eight; Basic Chord Theory

A **chord** is basically a simple thing. It is three or more notes stacked on each other.

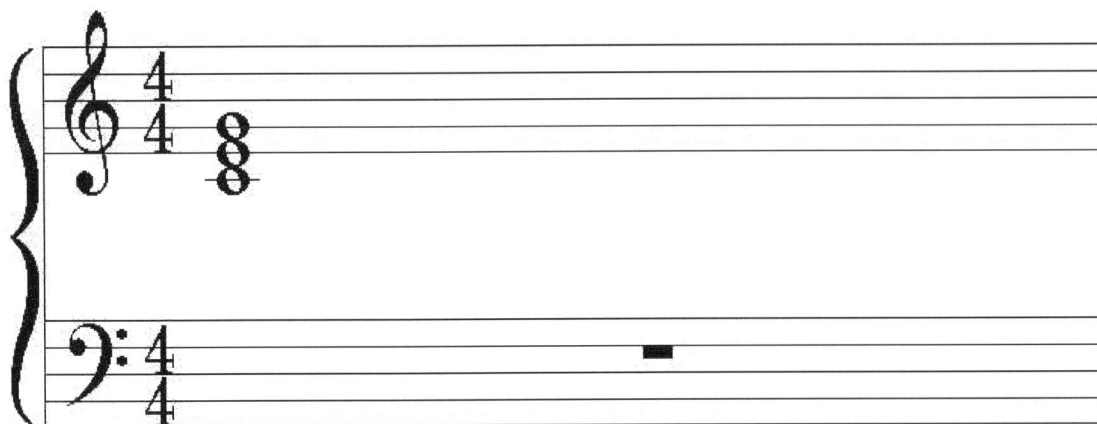

As you can see, the chord is constructed by using every other note. If the bottom note is **C**, the next note is **E** and the next note is **G**.

The bottom note is called the **root** and gives the **chord** its name. This is therefore a **C chord**. The next note is called the **third,** as that is the **interval** from that note to the **root**. The uppermost note then is called the **fifth** because that is the **interval** from that note to the Root.

A **chord** stacked in this basic way is said to be in **root position.**

More notes can be added to this basic **chord** by continuing to skip notes or letters;

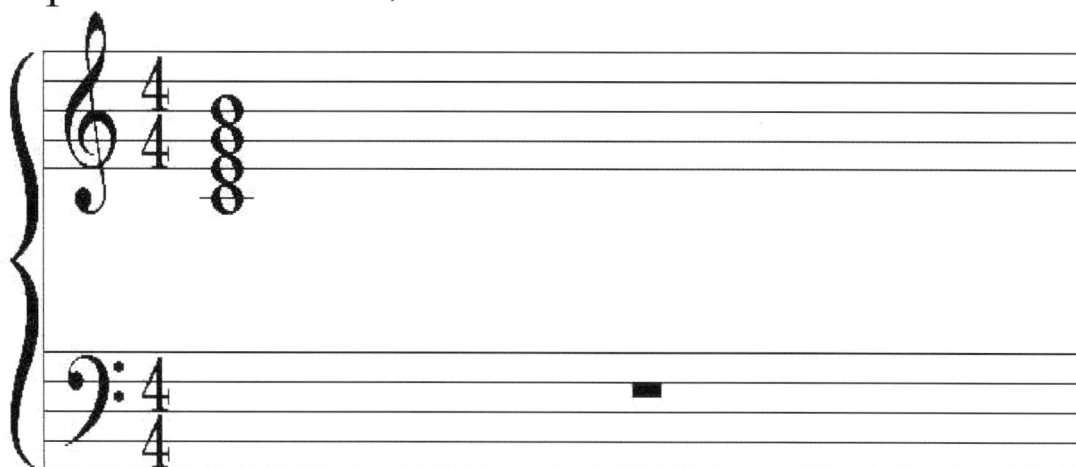

The fourth note of this **chord** would be called the **seventh,** as that is the **interval** from that note to the **root. Chords** with four notes are called **seventh chords.** This **chord** would be called a **C7**.

In any **major scale** there are seven different chords possible, using the notes of the scale for their **roots.**

I   ii   iii   IV   V7   vi   vii   I

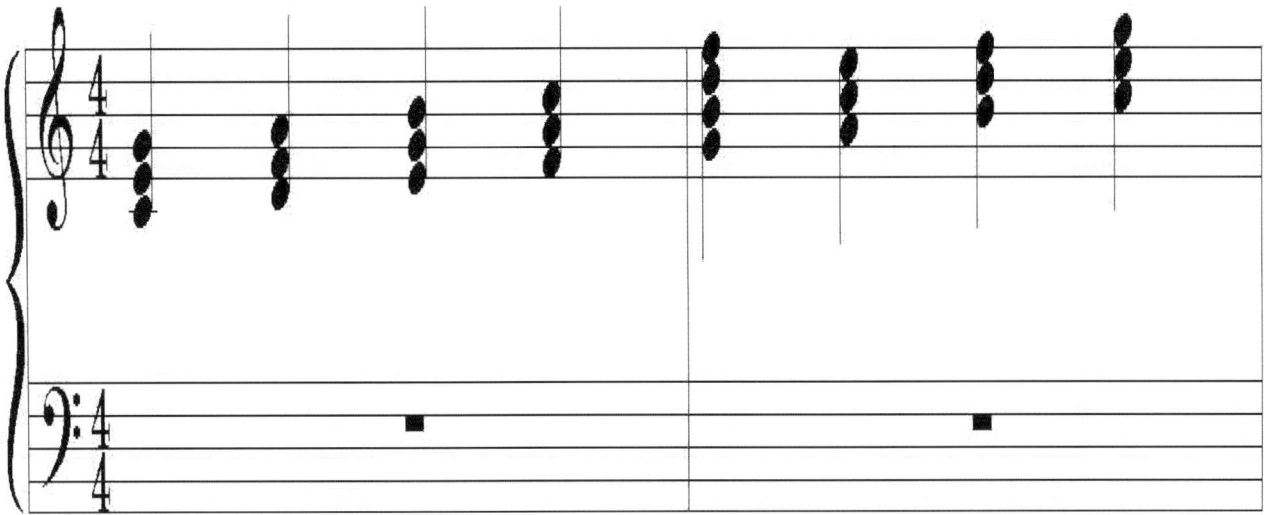

The **chords** can be identified by the **root** letter names; **C D E F G A B C**, but Roman Numerals are also often used. Each note of a **scale** gets a Roman numeral and the **chords** are identified by their Roman numeral.

The **V** or 5 **chord** is the one that most often and most traditionally gets a fourth note; hence it is the **V7 Chord**.

The **I, IV** and **V chords** are called the **primary chords** or the **blues chords** as I mentioned earlier in this book.

Now, to know what the **blues chords** are in any **key**, all you have to do is number the notes of its **scale** and pick out the **primary chords**.

The other chords of the scale are used quite a bit as well and are called the **secondary chords**.

Figured Bass

Chords hardly ever appear exclusively in **root position** as this would make for rather boring music.

Any **chord** can be **inverted** several times by simply placing the lowest note an **octave** higher.

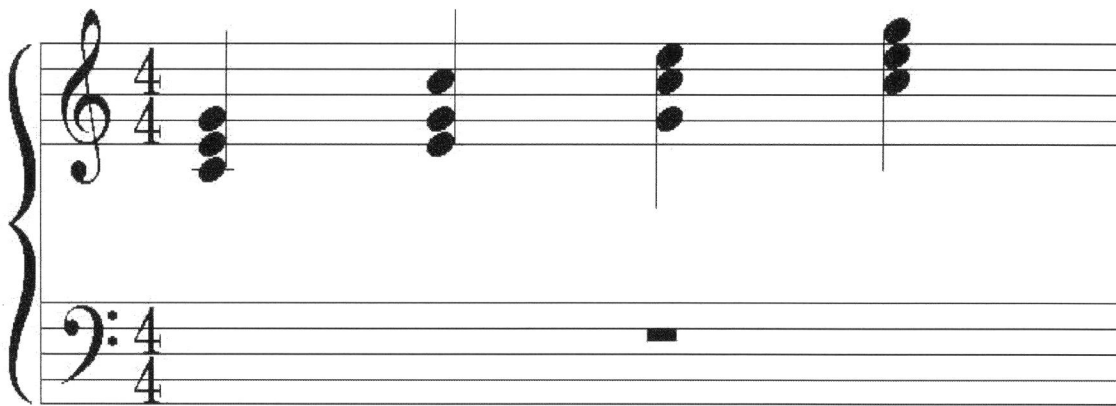

In the example above, the **C chord** begins in **root position.** In the next version of it, the **root** or **C** has simply been moved an octave higher. It's still a **C chord**; the **root** is just on top now. This is called **1st inversion**.

In the next version, the **third** or **E** has been moved an octave higher. This is called **2nd inversion.**

The final one shows the **chord** back in **root position** only it has now all been moved an **octave** higher.

In tracking what Inversion a **chord** is in, musicians use an old, old practice called **figured bass**. This is simply a method of showing the intervals of the Chord from the highest note to the lowest note.

The **root position** is often shortened to C5 and the First Inversion is often shortened to C6. Also, if no numbers appear, it is assumed to be **root position**.

Chords with four notes or **seventh chords** are inverted in the same way that three notes chords are, only you get three inversions instead of two.

Again, if no numbers are given, it is assumed to be **root position**.

A Short Description of the Long History of Figured Bass.

What has been described here is basically what appears in **chord** charts that are used to this day by Jazz and pop musicians. There is a bit more information given in the chord charts, which will be explained in the upcoming chapters.

Chord charts have been used at least since the sixteen hundreds. Back in the day, the groups were small, mostly strings and there was no conductor.

A keyboardist and a 'cellist sat together and lead the group and they read off of **chord** charts and improvised their parts.

The lowest notes they were allowed to play were whatever the lowest notes in the **chord inversions** gave, hence the term Figured Bass.

Block and Broken Chords

Chords may be played simultaneously, in which case the notes are stacked on top of one another, as we have been seeing them. These are called **block chords**.

The notes of the **chord** can also be played individually and this is a chord pattern or **broken chord**.

In this example, the **C chord** in measure one is a **block chord** and the **chord** in measure two is a **broken chord**. Measure three is a **broken chord** as well but this one, where the notes keep moving straight up (or down) through the octave is also known as an **arpeggio**.

Chapter Nine; The Qualities

Let us briefly review **intervals**.

The definition of the term *interval* is the distance between any two notes. The distance is counted by simply counting up the letters inclusively from one note to the next.

For example; C to G would be called a fifth because there are five letters from C to G (counting C and G); CDEFG.

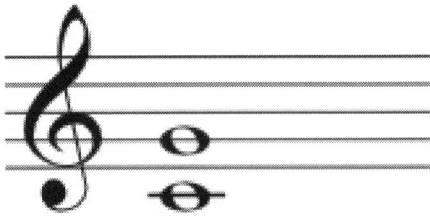

Interval of a 5th

In counting the interval on the staff, you would count the note you go from and then count every space and line until you got to the second note and count it as well. The above example would be called a *harmonic interval* since the two notes would be played simultaneously.

An interval can also be melodic, meaning the two notes would be played separately as in a melody;

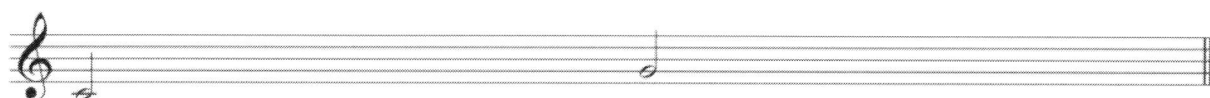

The Qualities

Since C to G would be a 5th but C to G flat would also be a fifth, there was needed a way to make a distinction between two such intervals. Hen ce the four *qualities*. The four qualities are; major (perfect), minor, augmented and diminished.

Major or perfect can be thought of as the default. They both mean the same thing except that the term perfect applies only to 4ths, 5ths and Octaves (8ths). What major or perfect means is that the upper note of the interval is found in the same scale as the bottom note.

For example; all intervals that have C as the lower note will give you major and perfect intervals as long as the upper notes are naturals;

M2   M3   P4   P5   M6   M7   P8

If, for example, the lower note is G, then you figure from the scale of G, which would mean you use an F sharp for the 7th since the key signature of G major has an F sharp in it;

M2   M3   P4   P5   M6   M7   P8

The following would be applied then, to get the other 'qualities;'

A major interval becomes minor by making it a half-step smaller and a minor interval becomes diminished by making *it* a half-step smaller. A major interval becomes augmented by making it a half-step larger.

A perfect interval become diminished by making it a half-step smaller, (there is no minor quality for perfect intervals.) Making it a half step larger augments a perfect interval.

Obviously there are several different ways to make an interval larger or smaller; you can flat the upper note or sharp the lower one to make it smaller and, conversely you might sharp the upper note or flat the lower note to make it larger. A note that is already flatted or sharped could be changed to a natural. For example, a perfect 4th of F to B flat could become augmented by making the B a natural.

Finally; major is designated by capitals, as in 'M3rd.' Minor is shown by lower case as in 'm2nd.' Augmented uses a plus sign as in '5+' and diminished uses a very small zero that resembles a degree sign.

Chapter 10; Determining the Qualities of Three Note Chords

We now apply the same criteria we used for determining the qualities of intervals to determining the qualities of three note chords, or **triads**, as they are often called.

First, our definition of Major; a chord is major if all three of its notes are found in the major scale of the bottom note or root.

How to determine the qualities of three note chords.

In this example, the root of the chord is C, so we compare the upper notes to a C Major scale and find that they fit in. The chord is therefore **major**.

Now, if you lower the middle note of a major chord by a half step, you get a **minor** chord; abbreviated 'min.'

If you take the minor chord and shorten it a bit further by lowering the top note, you get a **diminished** chord; abbreviated 'dim.' or a tiny little circle that looks like a degree sign.

Finally, if you take a major chord and increase it by making the upper note a half step higher, you get an **augmented** chord; abbreviated 'aug.' or a plus sign, as in 'C+.'

Qualities of Some Seventh Chords

Here are some common **qualities** for **seventh chords;**

CM7   C Dom7   c min7   c dim7

The first example is a **major seventh** chord, which is a **major triad** and a **major seventh**.

The next one is a very special chord called the **dominant seventh**. It is a **major triad** and a **minor seventh**.

The third one is a **minor seventh**; a **minor triad** and a **minor seventh**.

The last one is called a **diminished seventh** and it's a **diminished triad** and a **diminished seventh**.

Yes, there are two flats on that last **B**. This is called a double flat and it lowers the note a whole step. You can't just call it an **A** in this case, however, because that would mess up the spelling of the chord. Remember how chords are built by skipping letters? If you change a letter, you change the chord and then things get *really* confusing!

Now I said that the **dominant seventh** was a very special chord. It is the only naturally occurring seventh chord with a **major triad** and a **minor seventh** in any scale. It only occurs on the fifth or '**dominant**' note of the major scale.

You can make seventh chords out of any of the other chords in the major scale but they will all have different qualities and as soon as you change one into a **dominant seventh** by lowering the seventh, you've changed your **key**.

The dominant seventh's job is to lead you back to the 'I' chord.

If you see a dominant seventh that doesn't belong in the key, it's there to do its job as well, which is leading you to *its* 'I' chord. To find its I chord, just go down a perfect fifth and that will be the next chord in the progression. They are called '**barrowed dominants**' and they are used to change the key.

Dominant seventh chords are also used in the **Blues** and the primary chords are all turned into **dominant sevenths** for ease of improvisation. Don't fret! More on this later.

Chapter 11; Key Signatures and the Circle of Fifths.

A 'key signature' shows up at the very beginning of a piece of music, directly after the clef;

The key signature tells you two things; the name of the key and what flats or sharps, if any, are to be applied in the music. Flats or sharps that appear in a key signature apply to the entire piece, which is different than when they are used as **accidentals**.

There is a scale that goes with each key that starts on the same note as the name of that key. For example; for the key of **G Major**, the scale would start on **G**. Any sharps or flats that are in the key signature would apply to that scale. For example; the key of **G Major** has one sharp, which is **F**, so the scale of **G** would have an **F** sharp in it.

There is a system to the key signatures and understanding it makes using key signatures much clearer and easier.

The first step is to learn the order of the sharps and flats because they are always used in the same order;

The order of the sharps is **F C G D A E B**.

You can use the mnemonic; **Four Cats Go Dancing And Eat Birds** to help you remember this.

So, if a key signature has one sharp it is **F**;

If a key signature has two sharps, they will be **F** and **C**;

If a key signature has three sharps, they will be **F, C** and **G**;

And so on, always using the sharps in that specific order.
The order of the flats is; **B E A D G C F**.
The mnemonic you can use for this is; **Barney Eats   And Drinks Garbage Can Food**. (Hey, try coming up with a better one!)
So, if a key has 1 flat, it is **B**;

If a key has two flats, they will be **B** and **E**;

And, if a key has three flats, they will be **B, E** and **A**;

Lastly, all the keys are arranged in what is known as '**The Circle of 5ths**.' A 5th is an <u>interval</u>, so this is saying that each key is the interval of a 5th from the last one.

The 'Circle' starts with **C Major**, which is the only key that has no sharps and flats (all notes being **naturals**).   On the right side, the sharp keys go upwards by fifths and add one sharp each time.

On the left side of the circle, the flats go downward by 5ths, adding one flat each time.

It is important to note that these are **'perfect 5ths'** and so, for example, you go from **B** to **F sharp** and not **F natural** on the sharp side and you go from **F** down to **B flat**, not **B natural** on the flat side.

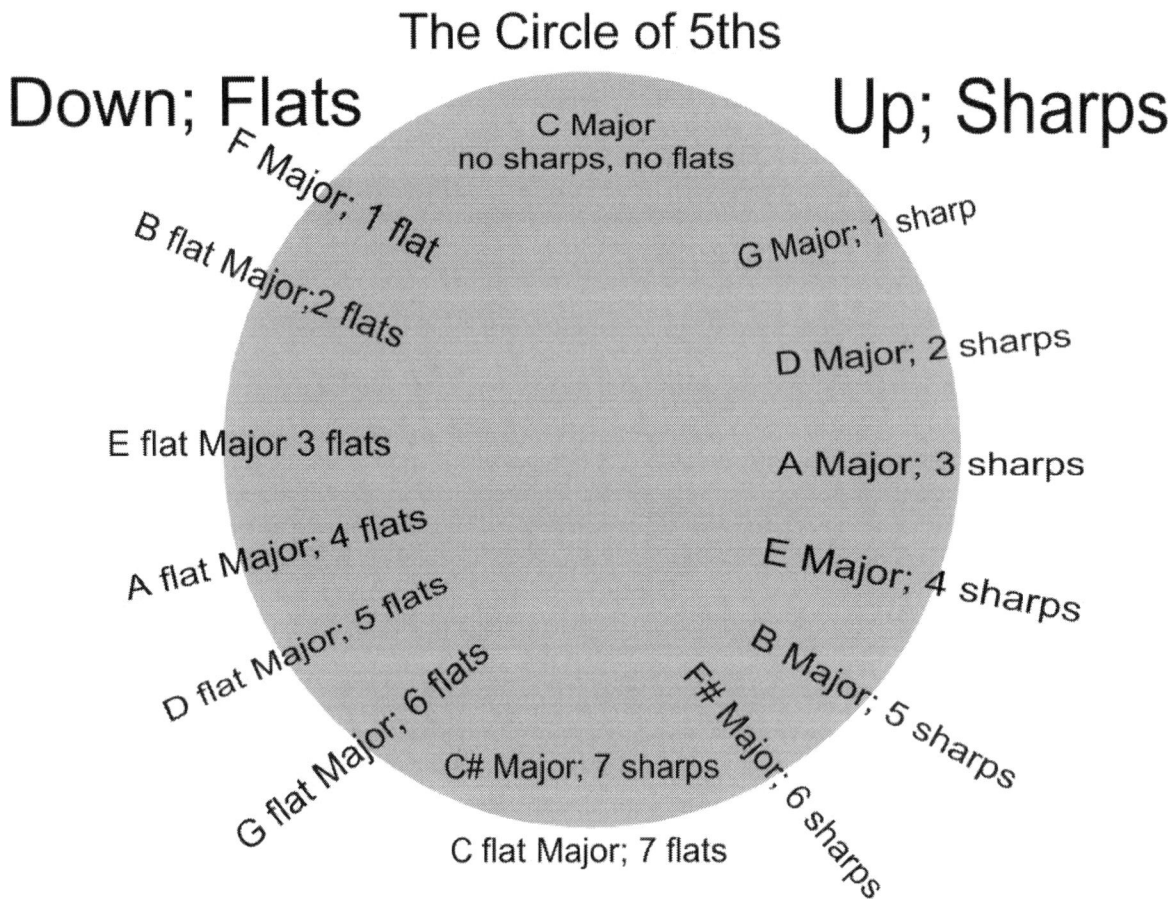

The Circle of 5ths

Down; Flats

Up; Sharp

C Major
no sharps, no flats

F Major; 1 flat

B flat Major;2 flats

E flat Major 3 flats

A flat Major; 4 flats

D flat Major; 5 flats

G flat Major; 6 flats

C# Major; 7 sharps

C flat Major; 7 flats

G Major; 1 sharp

D Major; 2 sharps

A Major; 3 sharps

E Major; 4 sharps

B Major; 5 sharps

F# Major; 6 sharps

There are a couple of short-cuts to reading key signatures, which were covered earlier, but the above information is still vital as you need to know what **sharps** or **flats** to apply to your music to be able to play in the right '**key**.' Practicing the corresponding scale to the **key** you are working in is the quickest way to master a particular key.

Chapter 12; Chord Progressions, Melodies and Phrases.

A **chord progression** is simply a series of different chords that a composer or songwriter uses in a song or piece of music.

Lets take a look at a very simple one.

I   I   V6   I   I

                             5

I   V6   I

            5

This is a very simple progression, using two of the primary chords; the **I chord** and the **V chord**, which is in **first inversion** and some of the notes omitted.

It is not unusual to omit some notes of a chord, especially the **V chord**. This does not effect the functioning of the chord.

Chord progressions can be simple, like this one, or complex.

Now let's add a melody on top of this same chord progression;

Merrily We Roll Along with Chords

There is a relationship between **melody** and the **chords**.

If you look in the first measure, for example, there is a **C chord**. A **C chord** has the notes **C E** and **G**. In the melody, you can find an **E** and a **C**. There are also two **D**s. These are **non-chord tones**.

A **melody** can have **non-chord tones** in it; in fact this is part of what makes it interesting but it needs to have predominantly chord tones to sound decent.

Another thing I want to point out is that this melody is eight measures. It's divided up into two phrases, each four measures long.

The two phrases are the same; they just end up a bit differently. (More on that in a minute.)

The two phrases can be the same or they can be different but nearly all melodies are eight measures.

If you are a songwriter or composer, this is not something you want to change around and expect to be successful; you can change a great many things in music, but the eight-measure melody is not one of them.

If you want to learn to write music, learning to turn out good eight measure melodies is a great place to start.

Cadences

Cadences are simply endings and putting two **primary chords**, one after the other, is how they are done. If you put the **V7** chord before the **I** chord, you have an **authentic cadence**. This is the most used **cadence** because it really sounds finished. The British call it the **perfect cadence**.

If you put the **IV** chord before the I chord, you get a warm, fuzzy ending called the **plagal cadence**. This is the 'Amen,' in church hymns.

If you end on the **V7** chord, you get a **half cadence** or **imperfect cadence**. This one leaves you hanging and doesn't sound finished.

The melody above has a **half cadence** at the end of the first phrase and an **authentic cadence** at the end of the second.

This is a common configuration of **cadences** in melodic **phrases** and it is called the **question and answer**, for obvious reasons.

The is also a **cadence** of the **V** chord going to the **vi** chord which is called the **deceptive cadence**.

Composers all know how important a good ending is so they always used the **authentic** or **plagal cadence** at the very ending.

I can only think of one composition that ends with a **half cadence** and that's Also Sprach Zarathustra by Strauss. He had a reason for doing so.

Chapter 13; Improvisation, Jazz, Blues and Other Scales.

The Theory of Consonant and Dissonant Intervals

Some **intervals** are said to clash or sound ugly when played together and some **intervals** are said to sound well or harmonize when played together.

The **intervals** that clash are called **dissonant** and the **intervals** that harmonize are called **consonant**.

As I've already pointed out, there is a relationship between **melody** and the **chords** in that **melody** must have predominantly **chord** tones or tones that harmonize with the notes of the **chord**.

The **melody** can have a certain amount of **non-chord** tones but, as long as this is balanced out with chord tones, the effect is still pleasing to most ears.

People will carry on about how Mozart's music has the perfect harmony but, in point of fact, there is quite a bit of **dissonance** in his music. This, of course is balanced out with harmonizing intervals and so the effect is pleasing.

The **dissonance** just gives it some edge. If music has no **dissonance** at all, it will put you to sleep in two seconds flat.

So here's the breakdown of **consonant** and **dissonant intervals**. It's pretty simple, really.

2nds, and 7ths are dissonant. The rest are consonant. This is very broad and general, as not everyone will hear it this way.

It's very subjective, of course, but nothing seems to be quite as uniformly subjective as music.

Improvisation

Improvisation is the art of creating a part where there is no written music there.

It is not, generally speaking, making any old thing up but it is generating a musical part based on something such as a **head.**

A **head** is just a **melody**, such as the example in the previous chapter. In **jazz**, the musicians will first play a **melody** or **head** just as it is written and then take turns **improvising** their own version of it.

Their versions need to sound reminiscent of the **head** so this means they, at least, need to be following the chord progression of the **head.**

They usually do so by following a **chord chart** with **figured bass** as was covered in the chapter on **chords.**

In **improvising**, they need to hit predominantly **chord tones** from the **chords** they are on in any particular part of the music.

This is where a good knowledge of **chords** and **scales** is helpful. If you know **chords**, you can quickly pick-out notes that belong to the **chord** in **improvising** a part.

The normal **major** and **minor scales** are not very useful in **improvising** as the last notes of the scale produce some very **dissonant intervals** with most chords. For example, the **C major scale**, when played over a **C chord**, will give you a **minor second** at the end of the **scale**, which is the most **dissonant interval** of all.

Some solutions have been developed.

In the **Blues**, the **primary chords** are all converted to **dominant seventh chords** and using a flatted seventh in the scale as well gets rid of this dissonant interval. There is still a 2nd at the end of the scale but it is now a major 2nd and not so nearly as jarring.

The **pentatonic** scale eliminates the **minor seconds** as well and makes **improvising** a no-brainer. As the name suggests, this is a scale with five different notes.

There is a major **pentatonic scale**, which is constructed by removing the fourth and seventh notes of the **major scale**.

Removing the 2nd and 6th notes of the **natural minor scale** makes the **minor pentatonic scale**.

Adding the **half step** in between the third and fourth notes of the **minor pentatonic scale** or the half step between the second and third notes of the **major pentatonic scale** makes the **Blues Scale**.

What is referred to as the **twelve bar blues** is simply four measure lines of each of the **primary chords**. The basic formula can vary somewhat but this is basically it.

Some members of the group such as the bass player and keyboardist will set up chord patterns using the blues or primary chords and the lead instrument, such as the guitar will improvise over these.

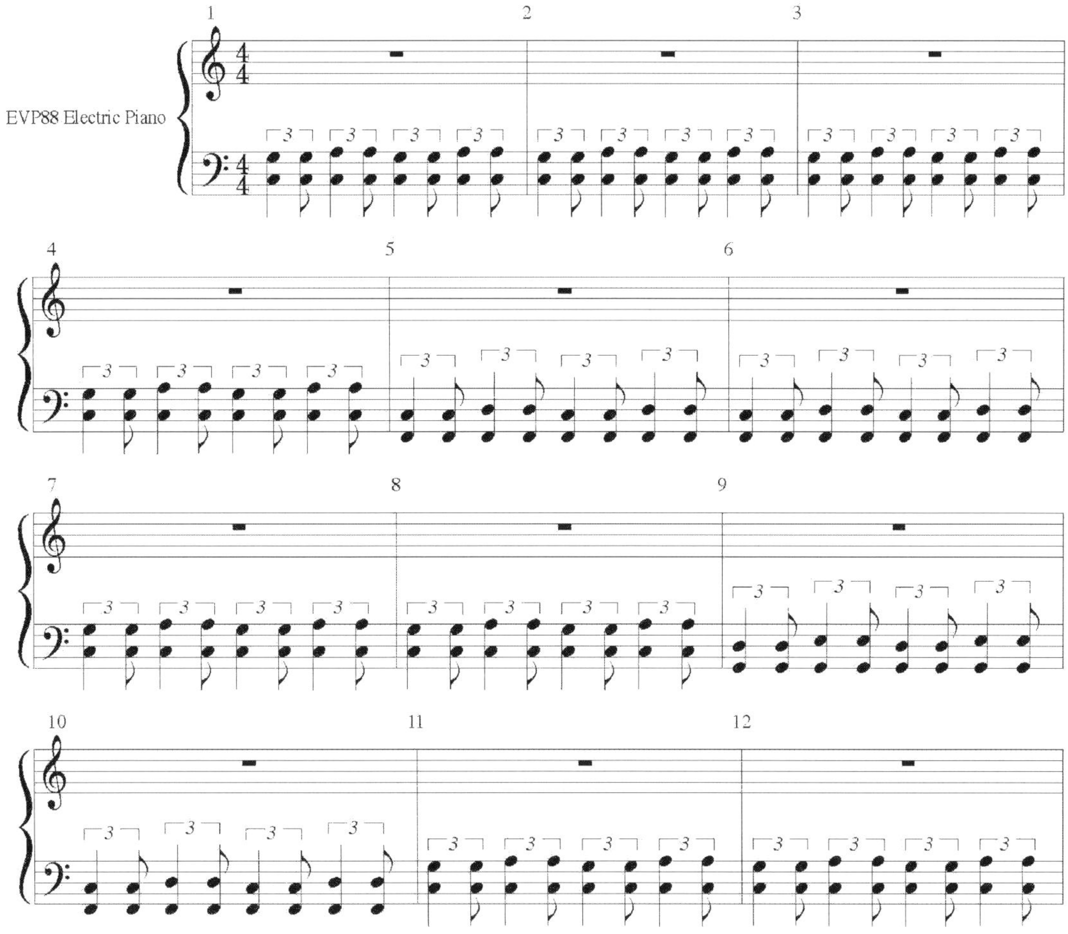

This is probably the freest form of improvisation.

The above example would be a **shuffle pattern**, meaning the rhythm is basically **triplets**. They are **eighth note triplets** only the first **two eighths** have become a **quarter note**.

Click on the link below, to listen to this example online.

You can see, that in this example, there are four **measures** or **bars** of the **I chord** followed by two **bars** of the **IV chord**, then two more of the **I chord**. Finally one bar of the **V chord** and one bar of the **IV chord** and then two more of the **I chord.**

Being in the **key** of **C Major**, the **I chord** is, of course **C**, the **IV** is **F** and the **V** is **G**. The chord pattern leaves out the **third** or **middle note** of the **chord** and the **fifth** or **top note** of the **chord** fluctuates back and forth between the true **fifth** of the **chord** and a neighboring **non-chord tone**.

A lead guitarist could easily improvise a part, using the **major pentatonic scales** that correlate to the **cords**.

In summary, **improvisation** is a skill that can be learned easily enough with a bit of knowledge about **chords** and **scales**.

The other part to this is **listening**. You need to listen to music in the style in which you are working in order to learn the **language** of that music.

Modes

Modes are just another type of **scales**. Some of the more common **modes** are; **Aeolian, Dorian, Ionian, Locrian, Lydian, Mixolydian** and **Phrygian**.

The **Aeolian Mode** is the same thing as the natural minor scale, or playing **A** to **A** on the white keys.

The **Dorian Mode** puts the half steps between the second and third notes of the scale and the sixth and seventh, like playing from **D** to **D** on the white keys

The **Ionian Mode** is exactly the same as a major scale, or **C** to **C** on the white keys.

The **Locrian Mode** has half steps between the first and second note and the fourth and fifth or like playing from **B** to **B** on the white keys.

The **Lydian Mode** has half steps between the fourth and fifth and the seventh and eighth, like playing white keys from **F** to **F**.

Mixolydian Mode gives us half steps between steps three and four and six and seven, like playing white keys **G** to **G**.

Finally we have the **Phrygian Mode** that gives us half steps between the first and second notes and the fifth and sixth, like playing the white keys from **E** to **E**.

The modes were obviously created by characters from a Greek play that didn't dig sharps and flats. By understanding where the half steps occur, however, you can **transpose** or move the scale to a new starting note at will.

Every type of scale has a specific pattern of whole and half steps and the difference between the different types of scales and the different chord qualities is obviously a small shift in where the half steps go.

Every major scale, for example, has half steps between the third and fourth notes of the scale and the seventh and the eighth.

Guitarists coined the term '**movable patterns**,' meaning a scale or chord pattern that can be moved to a different fret (note) and be played with the exact same fingering.

Well, every **scale** or **chord** in music is a **movable pattern** it's just on some instruments, such as the piano, it requires black keys and a different fingering but the pattern of whole and half steps for every **harmonic minor scale** remains the same, just as the number of **half steps** in any **minor third** is always the same and the **whole steps** and **half steps** between the notes of any **major chord** are always the same.

Modes are quite useful in getting a different sound for a composition. The chord changes can be especially fresh and interesting.

Chapter 14; Musical Forms

Form in music is the way a piece of music is constructed. We have already discussed a couple of the most important musical forms; the **melody** and the **Twelve Bar Blues**.

If you compared how music is put together with how a story or book is written, melody would be the equivalence of a sentence.

This is no coincidence as melody evolved from the song.

Melody is therefore the basic building block of musical form only, instead of many different melodies, musical forms tend to stick with a few.

Song Form has often been described as **A A B A** or **A B A**, **A** being the first melody and **B** the second melody.

This is a bit of an over simplification. Many songs have an **A** melody and then a **bridge**, which tends to be a bit of a melody in itself and then a third melody which is the **chorus**.

The **bridge** is often described as changing the **key** and this may or may not be true, depending on the song, but it does set up the **chorus**.

The first melody or the **verse** is usually the '**complaint**,' and the chorus is usually the '**answer**' or '**commentary**.' The **bridge** *introduces* the '**answer**.'

The longer, more 'complex' musical forms of the so-called 'classical music' were really just longer versions of this same idea. There were basically one or two melodic ideas that were developed a bit and then returned to.

In the late 'romantic period' a melody often represented a specific character and the music told a story, much like the modern movie music of our day.

Chapter 15; Interpretation, Dynamics and Articulation.

Interpretation is the deciding on and conveying of the emotional character of the music. All music has an emotional character and the same piece may change emotional character many times in its duration.

The composer my give hints as to the emotional character of the music such as its title or there may even be some commentary available.

Whether or not the title gives any indication or if the composer said anything about it, the performer must decide what emotional tone to bring out in the performance of the music.

Other clues can be such things as **tempo**, **dynamics** and **articulation**.

We have covered tempo already. **Dynamics** are the indications of how loud or soft different parts of the music should be.

Traditionally these are, once again, often in Italian. Some of the basic ones are;

p, which stands for the Italian word **piano** or **soft**.

f, which stands for the Italian word **forte** or **loud**.

Placing an **m** before either of these means **mezzo** or **medium**. Thus we have;

mp, medium soft or,

mf, medium loud.

More **p**'s or **f**'s can be added, making it very soft or very loud;

pp, **pianissimo, very soft**. Just add an '**issimo**' for each **p**. Same holds true for the **forte**; add an 'issimo' for each **f** .

Articulation is the way a note is played. Below are a few examples of some common articulations;

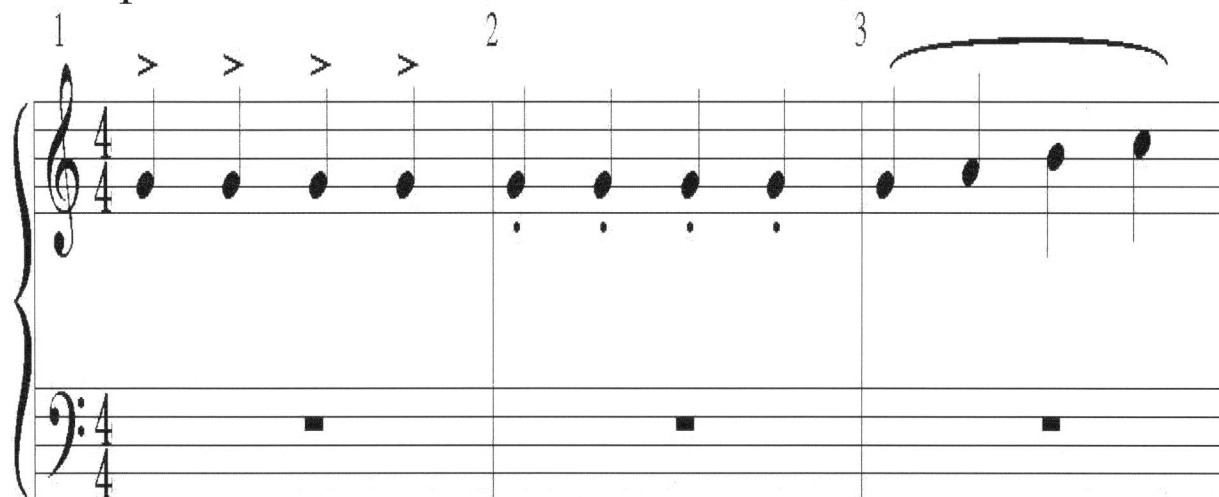

In measure one, the little arrow thingies above the notes are called **accents**. They mean to play the note that is accented louder or with a punch. Obviously used to convey a more fiery character.

The little dots above the notes in measure two are called **staccato** and this is an indication to play the notes crisply with a slight separation. This would make the music perkier.

The curved line above the notes in measure three is called a **slur**, (not a **tie** because it connects notes of *different* pitches.) This means to play the notes in a smoothly connected manner.

There are many other tempo, dynamic and articulation indications and I recommend getting a good musical dictionary for these. The 'Essential Dictionary of Music,' published by Alfred is a very good one.

Using the correct tempo, dynamic and articulation is a good way to get into the right character of the music.

You should not worry about whether or not you have the exact right interpretation that the composer intended as they often left this up to the performer's interpretation to a large degree.

Sure, you can be right out of the ballpark, so to speak, but it is better to have your own interpretation and be a bit off than to just copy someone else's.

So you should have an idea of what the music means to you and never play with an empty head. If you don't feel it, the listener never will.

Sometimes what can help is to start with a picture that the music conjures to you and work from there, deciding if the picture is sad, happy, heroic or whatever.

Chapter 16; Crossing the Great Divide

Once upon a time, I had a pretty good teacher.   Actually, he was the best teacher I ever had. He was a Hungarian violinist, extremely talented and very brilliant.

He taught me quite a number of things, one of them being, great musicians are not always great teachers.

The reason for this is that a lot of accomplished musicians started so early that they have forgotten a lot about how they do it. Some take it for granted that certain things are self evident in music.

When I started teaching I was quite taken aback when I queried a student and found he was looking at where the stem of the note ended as an indication of what letter the note was.

Now why *would* someone assume that every line and space on the staff was a letter and it was where the head of the note was placed that told what the note was?

If someone didn't know this very basic stuff, it would keep him or her from ever reading music.

That's why this book is crammed with so much very basic stuff because, if any of it is missing, a person is very handicapped in studying music.

Another thing this teacher did was telling me my playing of the Tchaikovsky Violin Concerto was rather pedantic and boring.

I went home and worked on my interpretation.

The next week, he said it was pretty sloppy, bad rhythm, wrong notes and such.

So I went home and worked on my technique to sharpen it up.

The week after that we were back to pedantic and boring.

This went on for, oh, a month or so, him chasing me back and forth from one side of my brain to the other.

Finally, he leaned back and said

"You know, you can do both." And he gave me an analogy of a split screen movie where the big screen was the emotion and the little screen was all the data you needed to run it; rhythm, notes etc..

Well, this worked for me and it changed my life. It changed how I heard and thought about music because, you see, they were meant to work together. One supports the other.

The emotional content of the music actually only makes sense in context with the rhythm.

Another way to get this to work is to take music theory out of the purely theoretical and apply it.

How do you apply it?

It's supposed to make playing music easier. This works by breaking down what you are doing into simpler patterns.

All music is made from scale patterns and chord patterns and these are as simple as it gets.

One analogy that I have used is looking up at the night sky and seeing millions of stars, or looking up and seeing the constellations.

The creator of the 'Far Side' comic once did a comic where a musician was sitting in the orchestra during a concert and saying to the one next him;

"Gee, look at all the little black dots."

Spotting the chord progression in a piece of music changes it from being lots of little black dots to something fairly predictable and manageable.

Most chord progressions are actually fairly simple and, knowing them brings some predictability since the melody needs to conform with the chord as we have examined earlier.

Music that sounds very complicated can often be reduced to a pretty manageable chord progression.

And this brings us to our final topic of memorization.

People often make the mistake of trying to perform with a note-association kind of memorization. That is to say, if they get one note, the next note will follow and so on.

So all it takes is one note to fall out of this house of cards. I can't count the number of times I've seen this memory technique fail, not because it has happened so many times but because it is so painful to see I've tried to suppress the memory.

One is usually witnessing the end of a music career.

In playing by memory, you need something you can hold on to that will be there when the adrenaline kicks in.

Once again, short of a photographic memory, chord progressions are good and any kind of pattern with the starting notes. Take a look at the music and see what kind of patterns are there. You may choose slightly different patterns than another musician studying the same piece but, if it works for you, that's what's important.

If you follow the advices in this book and learn to read using scale patterns and intervals and take some time to learn to recognize chords, this whole process will become fairly automatic and you will find that you know a piece by memory just in the course of having learned it.

How to Practice

I promised you, at the beginning of this book, I would teach you how to practice less and get more out of it. So here's a summary of how the material in the book should be applied.

This book contains all the basics you need to make lessons on any instrument work. Of course you should still take lessons on the instrument you want to learn, it's just that, if you apply the material in this book, especially in the beginning stages, you are certain to succeed in learning your instrument.

Remember these are the things that many teachers expect you already know or gloss over because of their extreme focus on the techniques of their instrument/

Or maybe they're just a lazy bozo. Armed with this book you will be able to tell if you are getting your money's worth

1. Learn your rhythm first. Use the drills and any others you can find in other books just as prescribed in the chapter on rhythm.

2. Go over the basic theory and pay special attention to the tips on making reading easier by using note direction and intervals. Make sure you understand all the definitions correctly. Use the glossary in the back of this book and get a good music dictionary because there are many, many other musical terms. Every time you come across a new musical term, look it up.

3. Learn to play scales. A simple scale such as the C major scale is good to start and should be the first one since this is where the naturals live and you won't dig sharps and flats unless you know where all the natural notes are on your instrument. Use a scale as a warm-up, playing it with a metronome using various rhythms. However much time you have to practice, a third of it should be spent on scales.

You can also practice chords from the scales you play as warm-ups. These are best done in arpeggio form. There are many good books that have scales and chords with fingerings all worked out for your instrument but it can be very profitable to work out your own fingering for these as well.

4. When you first learn a piece of music, apply counting to the rhythm in it the first couple of times you play it. People think, 'I'll learn the notes first and then put in the rhythm.' WRONG! *That day never comes! May as well say 'I'll build a house and put the foundation in later.' Nothing done this way will pass an inspection and you'll develop bad habits that will hold you back for the rest of your short musical career!* If you apply counting in the beginning, you will cut down the time it takes you to learn a new piece drastically because you won't have to go back and try to correct it later and you will develop the habit of playing music correctly the first time you play it. Also put dynamics into the music the first time as well. When you encounter a particularly difficult passage, drill it by playing it as a stand-alone section of the music. Play it a number of times, first slowly then gradually increasing the speed.

5. Practice sight-reading a few minutes each day. That is to say play an easy piece of music you have never worked on. Apply counting to it. Learn to pick out chords, scales and cadences in things you play.

6. If you plan to be a jazz or pop musician, double the time you spend on scales and chords.

Sight Singing and Ear Training

One of the things that dropped out, in traditional music training, when it came from Europe to this country was a little subject called sight singing and ear training.

You can still get it but it's usually a separate subject again.

It's basically learning to sing scales, intervals, chords and melodies (at sight.)

The ear training part is learning to identify these same elements from hearing them.

Again, a bit of this is highly profitable. Discerning pitch is in the mind; there is nothing physically different about a person's ears that make them better at distinguishing notes than someone else.

Contrary to popular think on this subject, you are not stuck with a certain ability to hear pitch. It can be changed and improved on.

If you play a variable pitch instrument such as a violin, being able to hear pitches correctly in your head is virtually a must. Even if you have a fretted instrument, you'll need to tune it.

You start this with easy things like learning to sing or hum a major scale. This is usually done with neutral syllables, although some people use what is known as solfeggio.

This is where C is called Do. Then the progression is do re me fa sol la ti do, being C D E F G A B C.

To do the sharps, change the syllable by changing it to an 'i.' Thus do becomes di with the 'I' being pronounced as 'ee.'

The flats are made by using an 'e,' which is pronounced 'ay,' thus ti becomes te. The only exception is re, which becomes rah.

Actually the hearing and singing become pretty synonymous. If you can sing something you can certainly hear it and visa-versa. If you can't hear it, you certainly can't sing it.

Finding familiar melodies that begin with the interval in question can assist learning intervals. For example, the bridal march (Here Comes the Bride,) starts with a perfect fourth.

If you find a familiar melody that begins with a seventh, come to the website and message me with what it is.

After awhile, you will be able to look at a melody and hear it in your head, which greatly speeds up learning new music and also a great skill to have if you're a composer.

Glossary

Here is a glossary of music definitions;
This list of music definitions is for musical terms used on the earlier levels.

1. Accidentals; an accidental is a sharp, flat or natural that is used in one measure. The accidental does not appear in the key signature and it applies to the particular pitch it is used on, in all octaves but only for that measure.
2. Arpeggio; An arpeggio is a broken chord, that is to say the notes of the chord are played individually, usually straight upwards or downwards, cycling through the notes of the chord.
3. Bar; another term for measure. The vertical lines that are seen in a musical score divide the music up into bars or measures and they contain the same number of beats as indicated by the time signature.
4. Bar line; the lines that run vertically in written music and divide the music up into measures or bars.

5. Bass Clef; Also known as the F clef, it is found usually at the very beginning of a piece of music and shows where Middle F is (the first F below middle C)

6. Beam; When 8th notes or the next smaller note values are connected with a single line, they are said to be beamed together.

7. Beat; The steady, rhythmic pulse that determines the speed or tempo of music.

8. Broken Chord; When the notes of a chord are played individually in any pattern.

9. Chord; A group of three or more notes built on a particular note and then added by skipping letters in the musical alphabet.

10. Circle of 5ths; the arrangement of key signatures.

11.Clef; a symbol used at the very beginning of music, usually, and each clef designates which notes of the musical alphabet are assigned to which lines and spaces on the staff.

12.Common Time; 4/4 time, indicated by a C where the time signature goes.

13.Crescendo; to gradually get louder.

14. Degree; what a note of a scale referred to as.

15.Diatonic; Notes found within a major or minor scale.

16.Diminished; smaller.

17.Diminuendo; to get gradually softer.

18.Double Bar; two bar lines together, usually marking the end of a piece or section.

19.Dynamic Markings; the symbols that indicate the loudness or softness that a piece should be performed at.

20.Eighth Note; A note that is half a beat or two 8th

notes equaling 1 beat.

21.Eighth Rest; a rest that is half a beat.

22.Fourth; an interval of a fourth or four letters apart.

23.G Clef; another name for the treble clef, since it locates G on the staff.

24.Half Note; a note that gets two beats.

25.Half Rest; a rest that gets two beats.

26.Half Step; going to the closest possible note either up or down.

27.Key; shown by the key signature, indicates that one note is the 'home note' or 'tonic.' Simply put, the note the piece must end on in order to sound finished.

28.Key Signature; shown at the very beginning, right after the clef, usually; it shows how many sharps or flats are in the key. Also tells what that key is called.

29.Major Scale; the scale that corresponds to the name of the key. It starts on the note that is the name of that key and has whatever sharps or flats in it that that key does. It is all whole steps except between the 3rd and 4th degrees and the 7th and 8th, which are half steps.

30.Natural; a note that is not a sharp or flat. C major has no sharps or flats so you can say that natural notes are those found in the key of C Major.

31.Octave; an interval of an 8th. Octaves will give you the same letter and most standard scales have at least 8 notes or an octave.

32.Pentatonic Scale; a scale that has only five notes or letters in it and usually avoids half steps.

33.Quarter Note; the note that gets one beat.

34.Quarter Rest; the rest that gets one beat.

35;Rest; there are rests that correspond with each note type. the corresponding rest gets the same duration but it is a duration of silence.

36.Rhythm; how notes of different duration are played against a pulse or steady beat.

37.Scale; in it's most general sense, a scale would be any time notes go up or down with no skipping of notes. More specifically a scale is usually 8 notes in a row and named after the note it starts on, e.g. CDEFGABC

38.Scale degrees; the names and numbers given to each note in a scale; I is Tonic, ii is Supertonic, iii is Mediant, IV is Subdominant, V is Dominant, vi is Submediant, vii is Leading Tone.

39;Second; interval of a 2nd, also called a step.

40.Staff; the group of 5 lines and 4 spaces that notes are written on.

41.TAB; abbreviation for Tablature.

42.Tablature; a popular notational system for guitar and other stringed instruments.

43.Tempo; the speed of the beat.

44.Time Signature; the two numbers at the beginning of a piece. The top number indicates how many beats are in a bar or measure and the bottom number tells what kind of note gets one beat.

45.Treble Clef; also called the G clef because it shows where treble G is on the staff.

46.Whole Note; the largest note. It gets 4 beats.

47.Whole Rest; the rest that gets four beats. This rest also means to rest an entire measure so, if the measures have three beats, this rest is then only three beats.

48. Whole Step; going from one note to the next with a sharp or flat in between. Two half-steps make a whole step. These are some of the most used music definitions on the earlier levels.

25541725R00060

Printed in Great Britain
by Amazon